# The Color Companion
# Pocket edition
# of

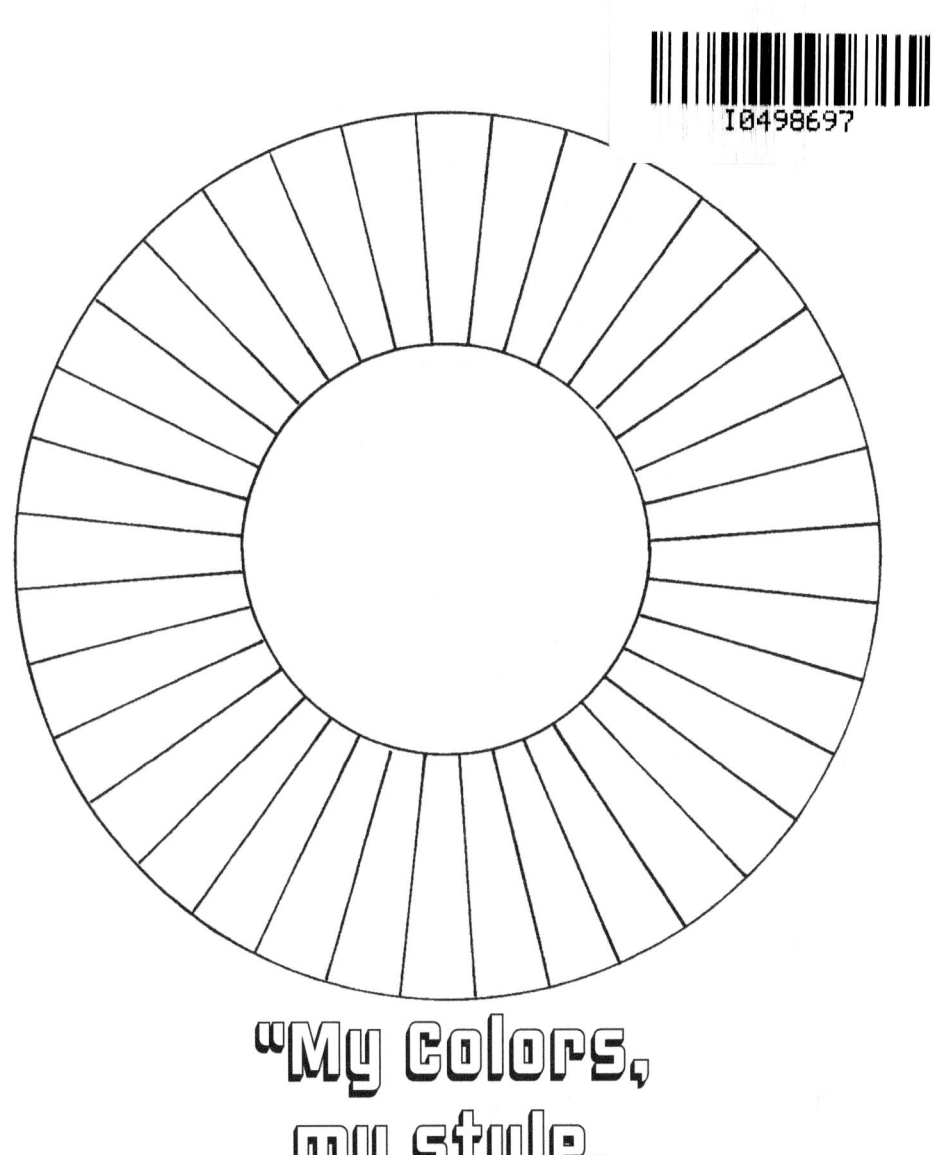

# "My Colors,
# my style,
# my way!"

## Share your colored versions with us !

The Official FB book page, stay on top of what we have in the works !
www.facebook.com/globaldoodlegems

The Community group, share your colored pages, meet the artists, enjoy exclusive freebies, take part in community Charity books and so much more......
www.facebook.com/groups/globaldoodlegems/

Follow us on Twitter.... @GlobalDoodlegem

We are on Instagram too
@globaldoodlegems for instagram

...and if you are not social like that we have a blog
globaldoodlegems.wordpress.com

Copyright © 2016 Global Doodle Gems
Published by Global Doodle Gems
  Anna-Marie Vibeke Wedel

All rights are reserved by Global Doodle Gems.

Duplication of pages for personal use are allowed.  You are invited to color the pages then scan/post your coloured versions to social networks, mentioning the book title and author/artist
(Global Doodle Gems).

All artwork and images are protected by copyright laws.  This book or any portion thereof may not, otherwise, be reproduced and/or distributed or transmitted without the express written permission of the artist/publisher of Global Doodle Gems.

All of us from the Global Doodle Gems wish you a colortastic time and look forward to seeing your wonderful color results online !

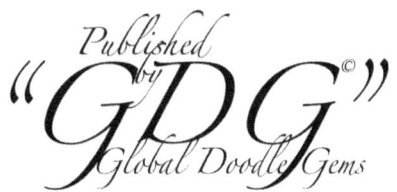

My Color Companion, the idea for this book, comes from my own need to always keep records of my colors, it is the first thing I do, when I get new pencils, markers or pens, as an artist I also test fineliners and pencils, I have handdrawn the 15 different templates inside this book ( each template is repeated 4 times in the book) , I recommend that you use a piece of cardstock between the pages when you test markers. The book is printed on the same paper as 90 % of most of the coloring books you will find on Amazon, which means it is a great place to test how your colors will work in the books, and create your own unique color palettes that are your style.
The mini edition is thought to be your companion on the go, a smaller size, easier to bring along on short trips ! Also check out the Biggie edition with 30 different templates (also repeated 4 times each giving you a whole 120 single pages to work with your colors on).

A big Thank you to my friend Johanna Ans for her great help with the creation of My Color Companion, be sure to follow our blog to get unique tip and ideas of how to use your color companion
globaldoodlegems.wordpress.com

*Maria Wedel*

# Table of contents

Template 1 Big Color Wheel 2x 72 spaces

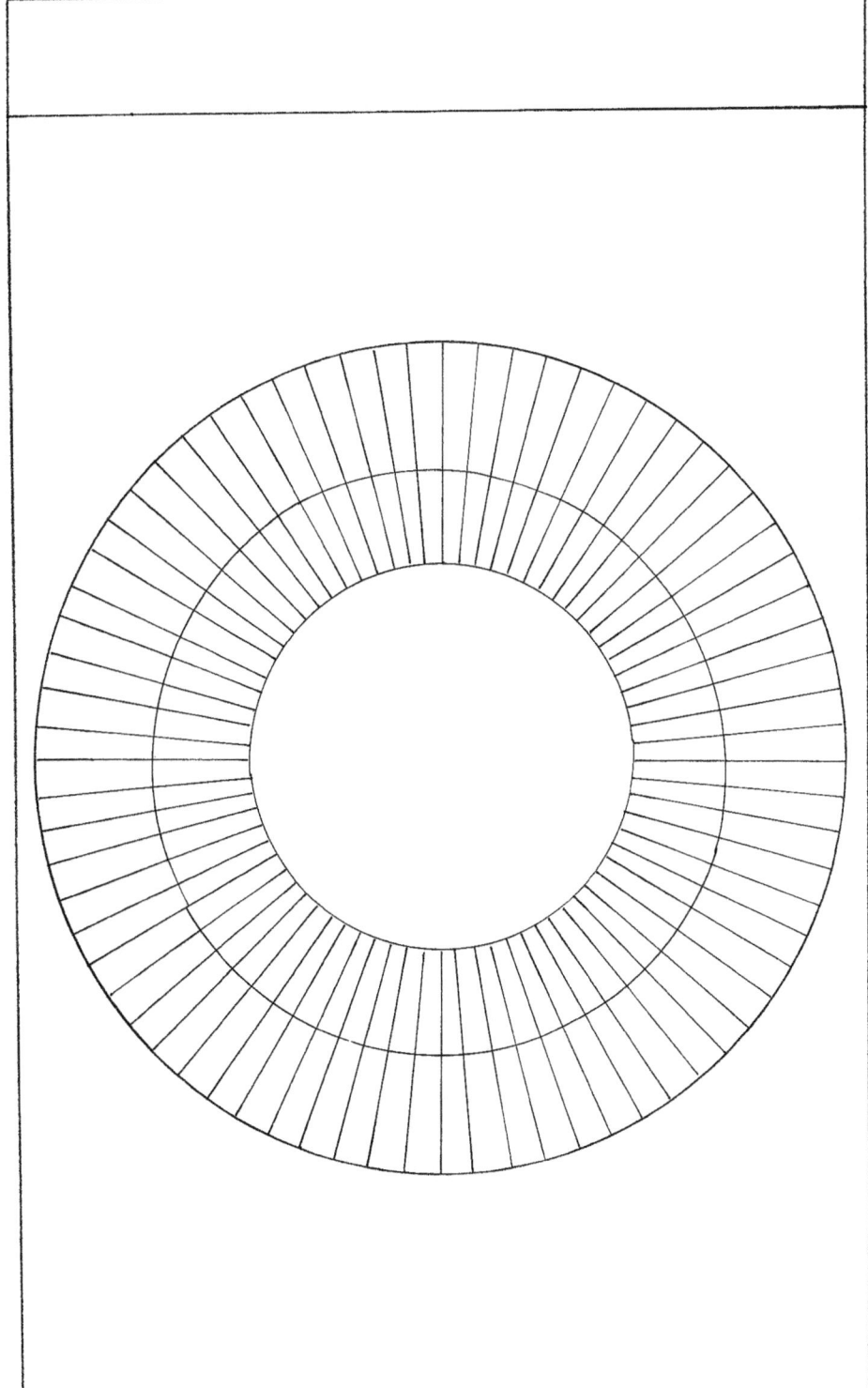

Template 2 Big Color Wheel 36 spaces

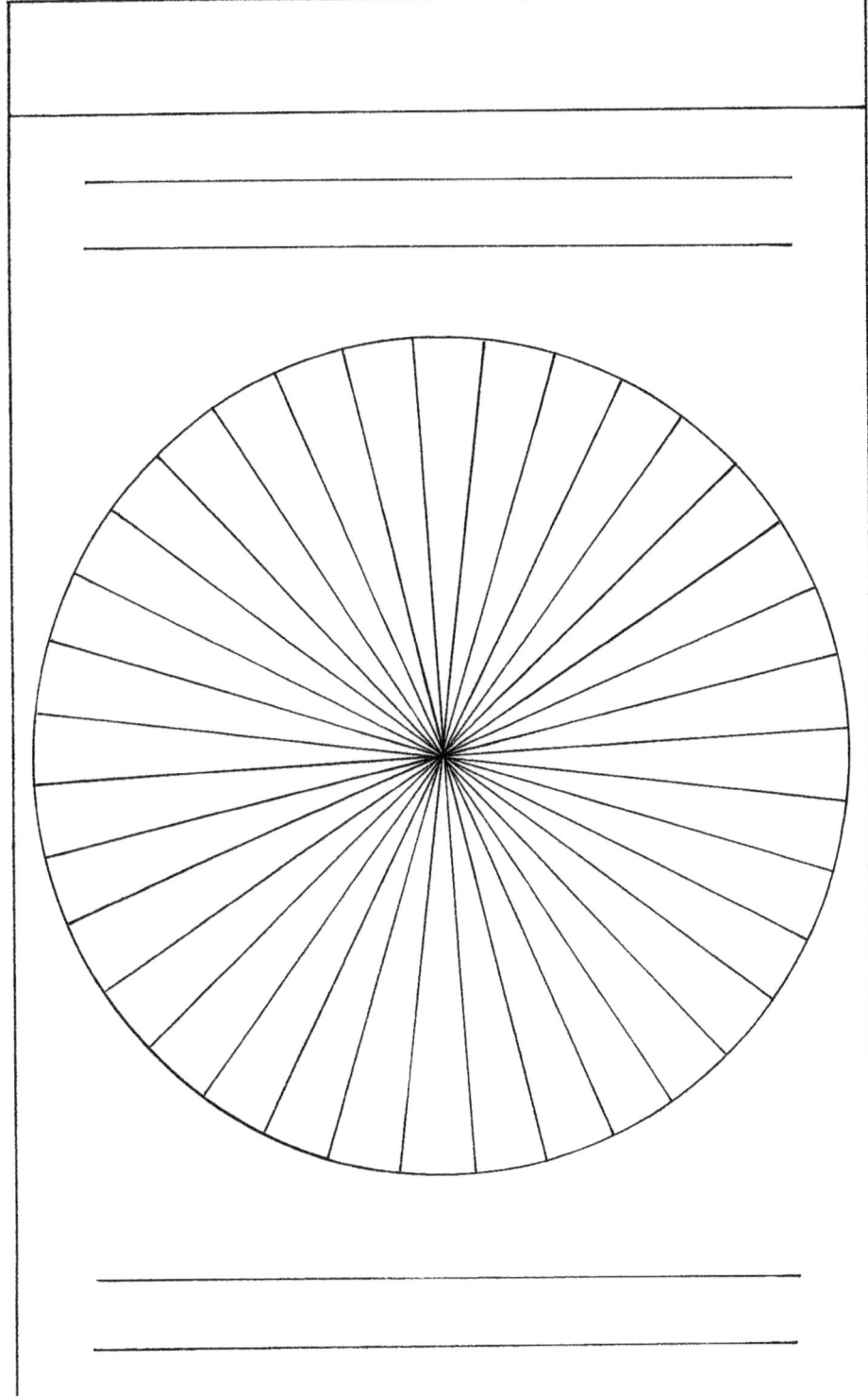

Template 3 Big Color Wheel 2x18 spaces

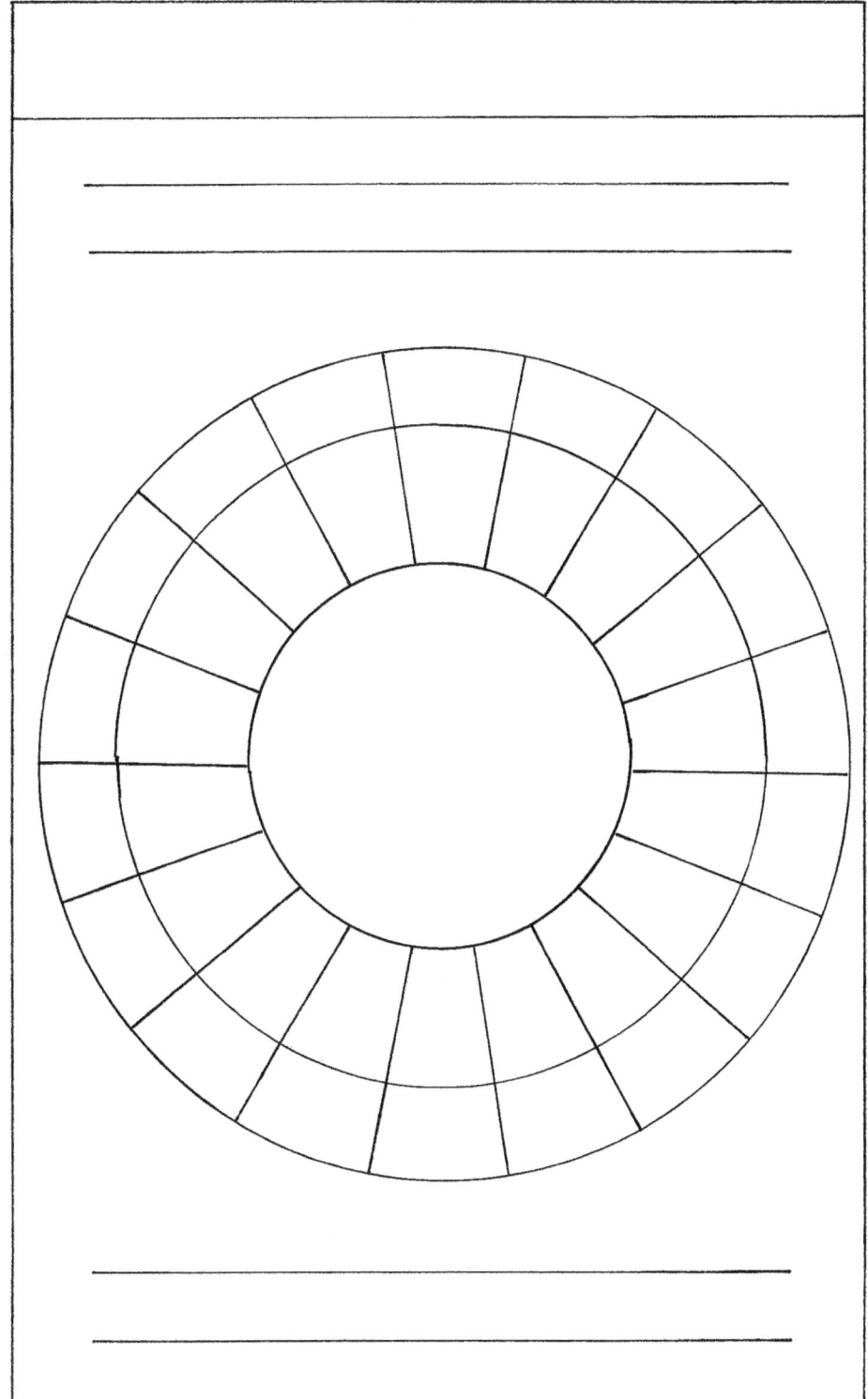

Template 4 Big Color Wheel 36 spaces

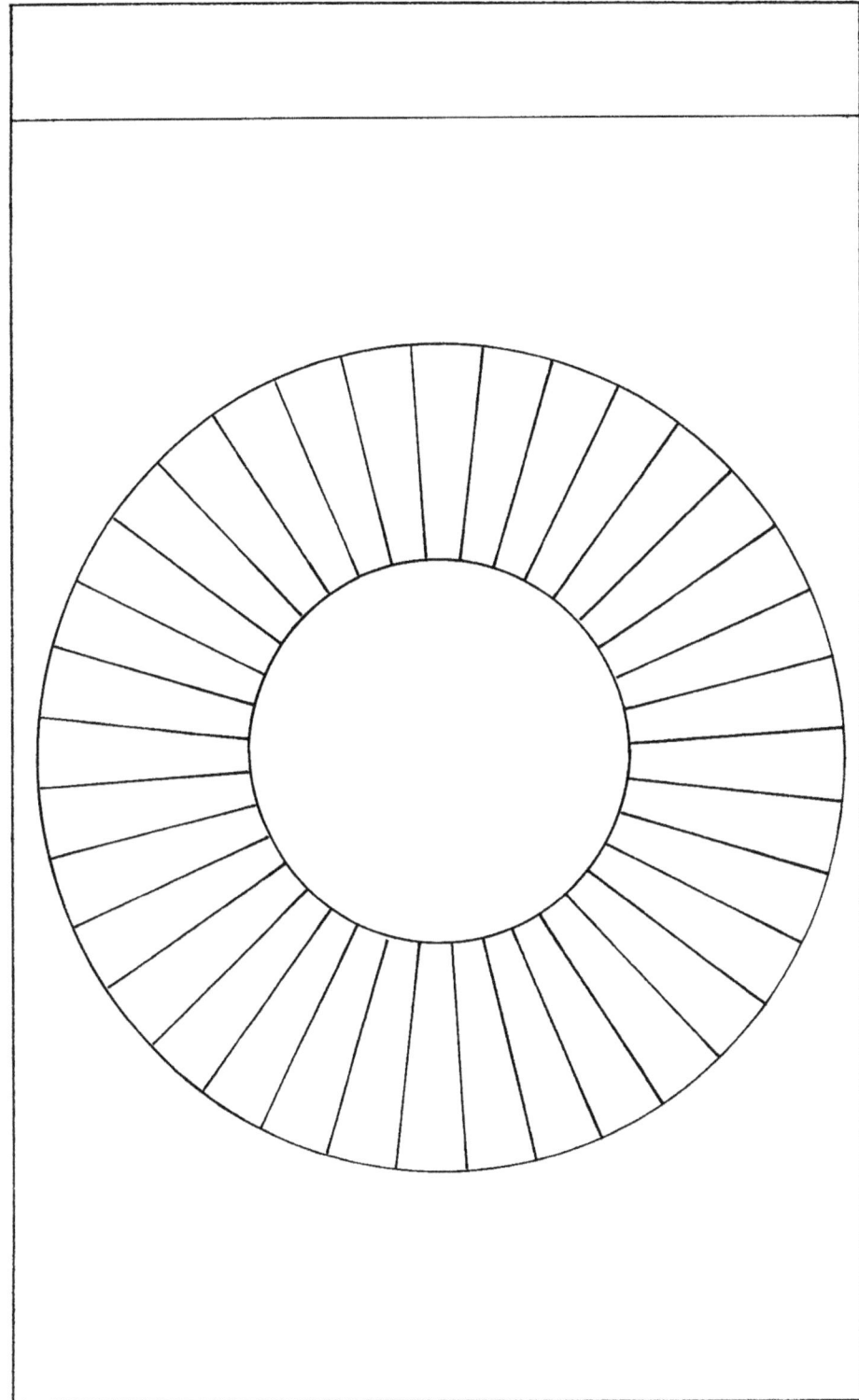

Template 5 15 blogs of 6 spaces

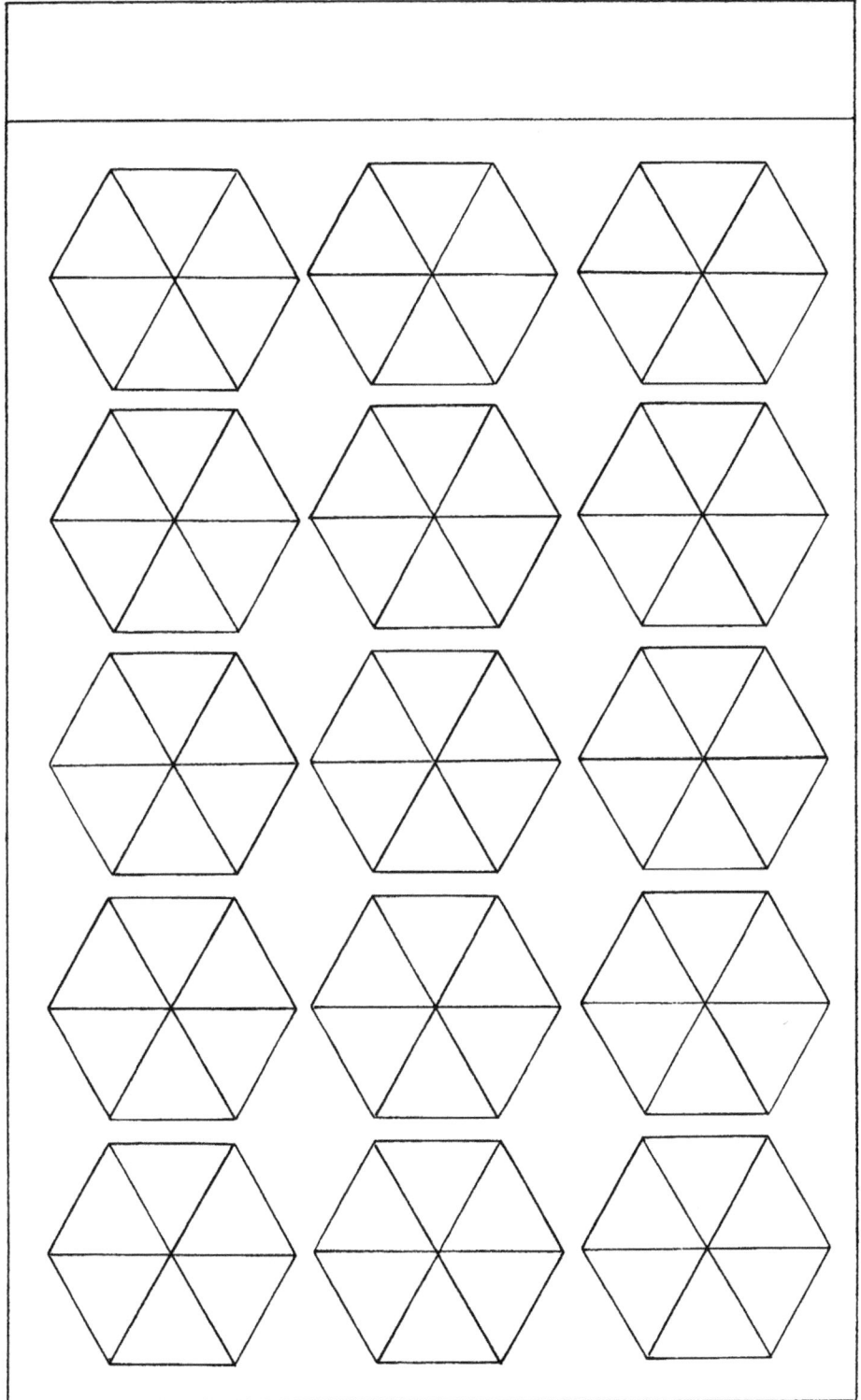

Template 6 6 squares of 4x6 spaces

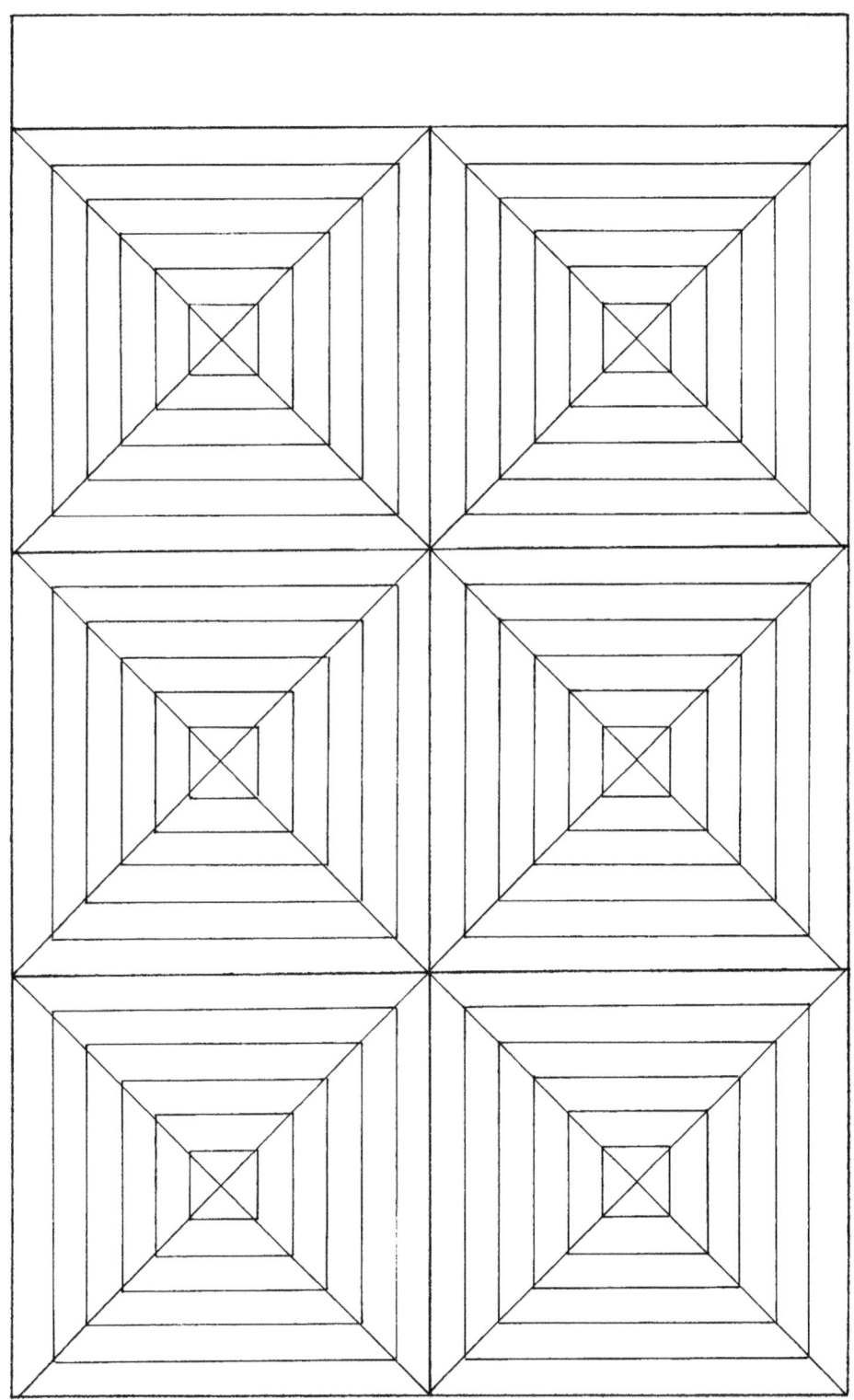

# Template 7 endless possibilities

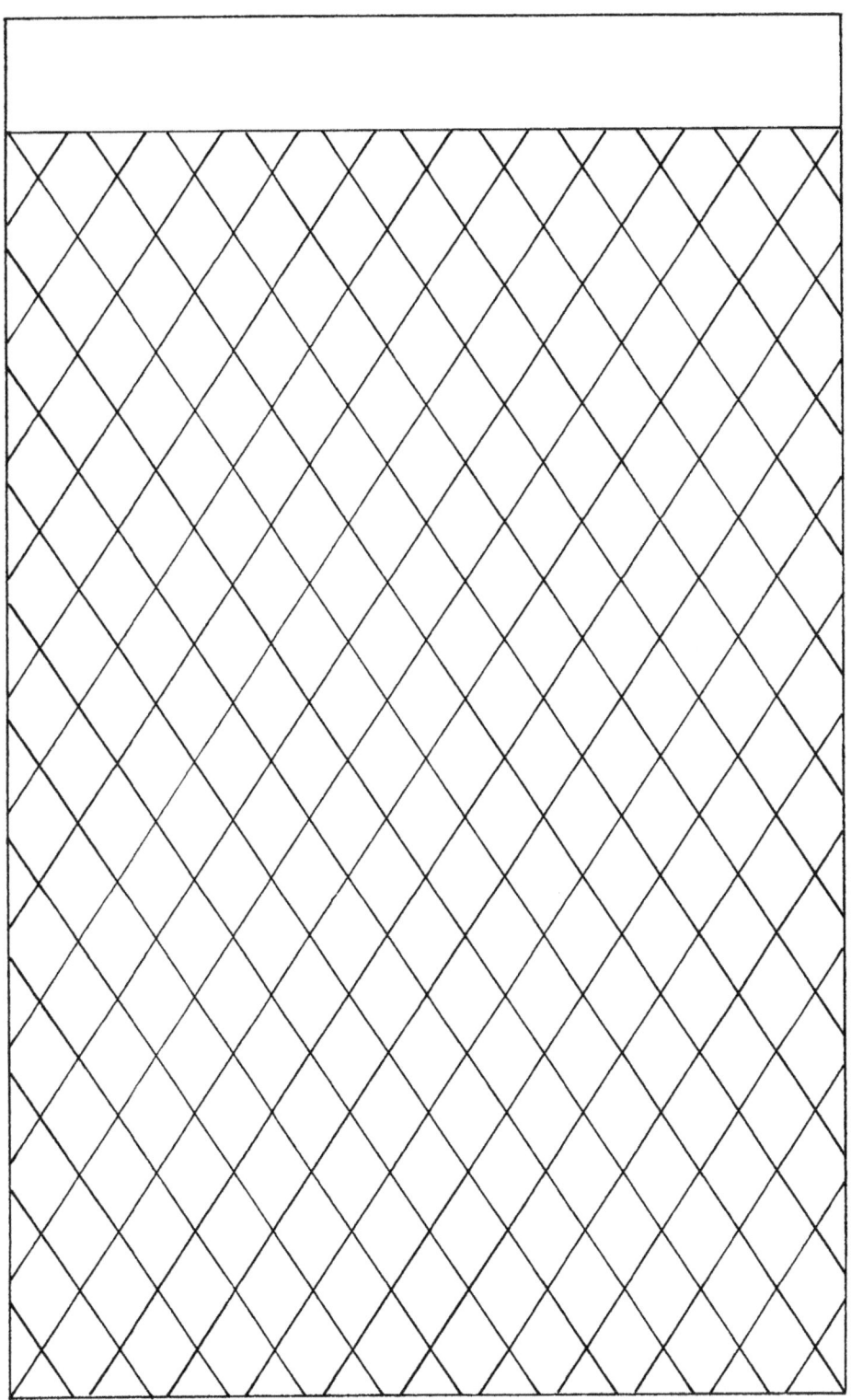

Template 8 6 lines of 32 spaces

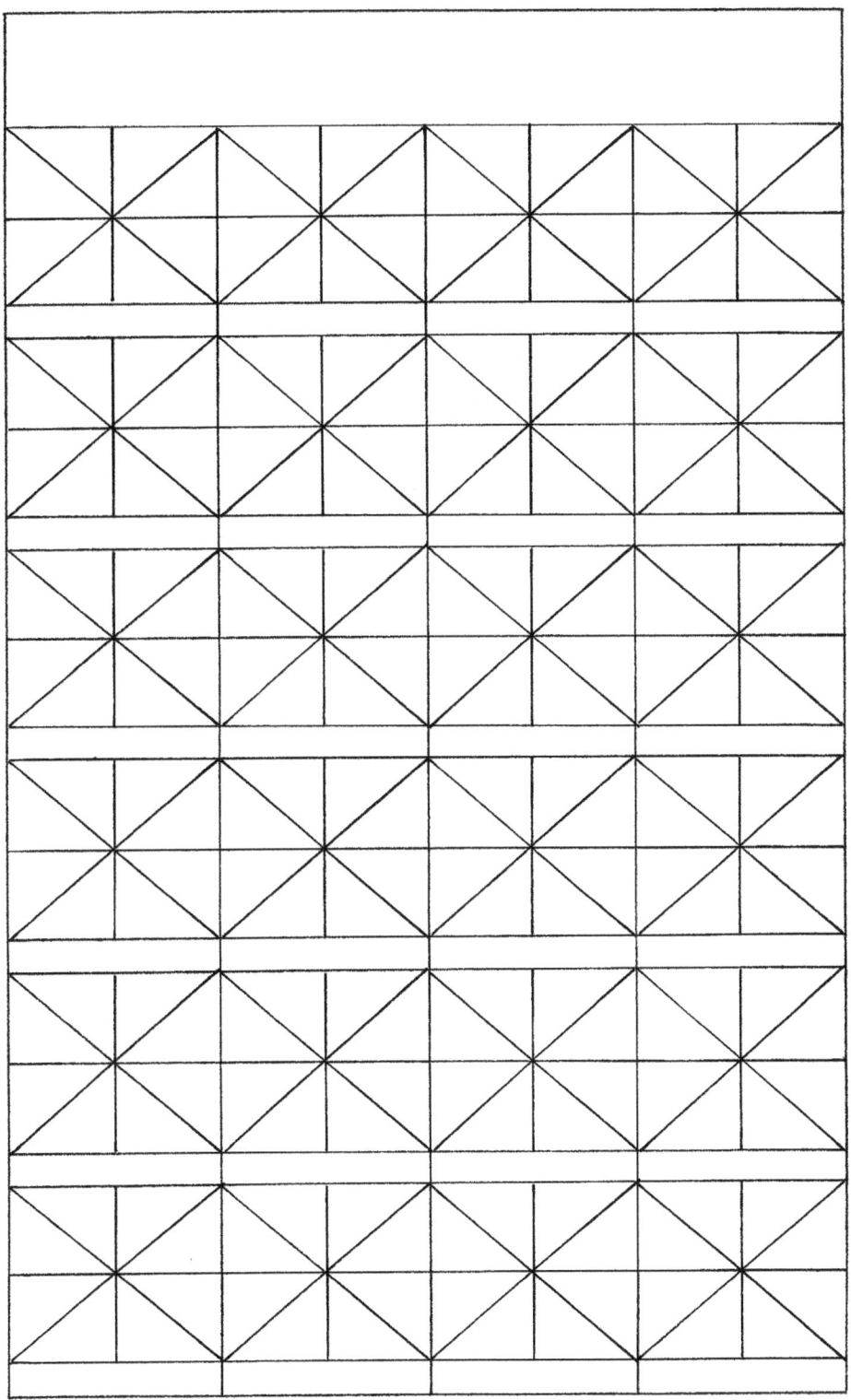

Template 9 6 lines of 24 spaces

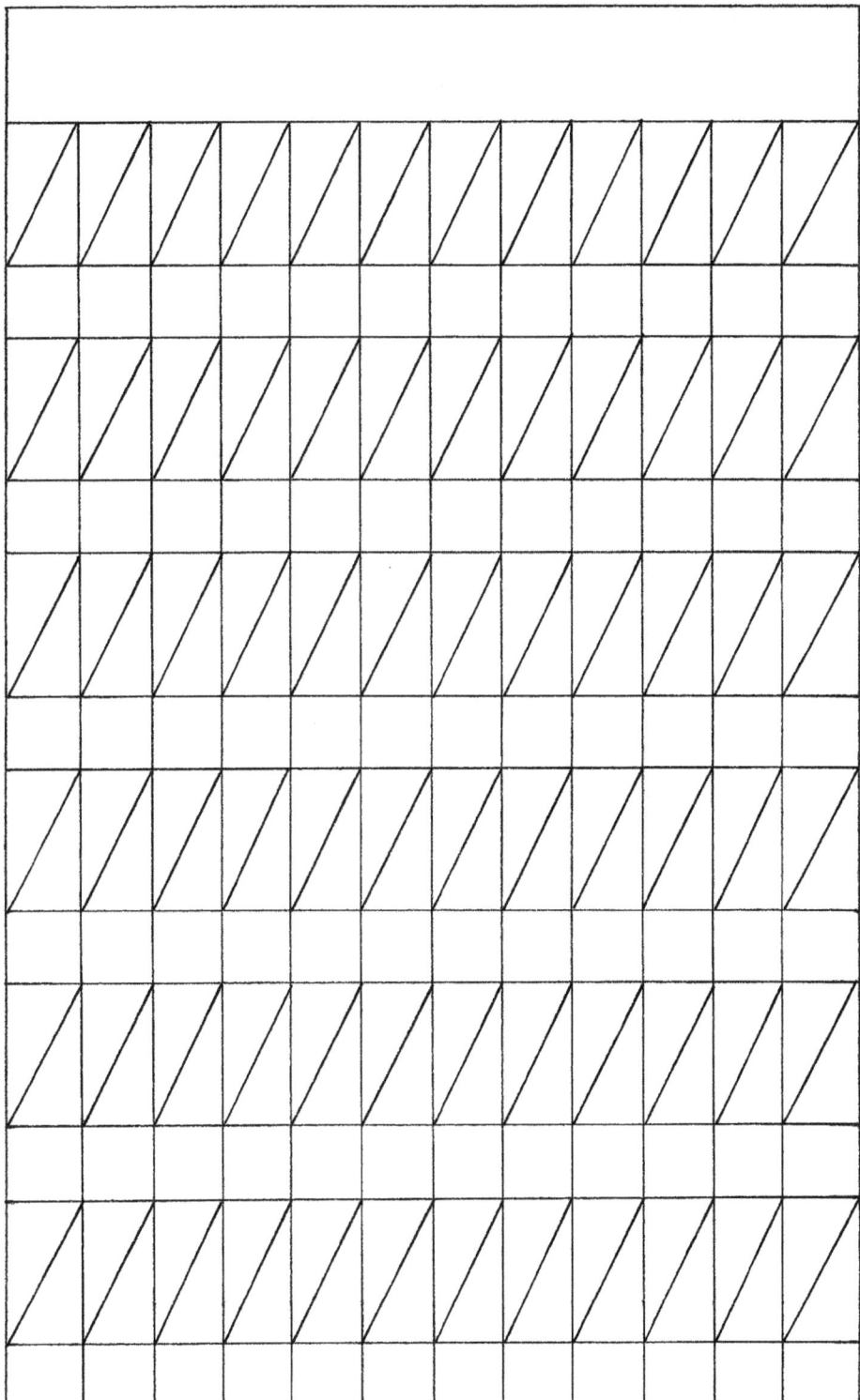

Template 10 Color Wheel 12 spaces

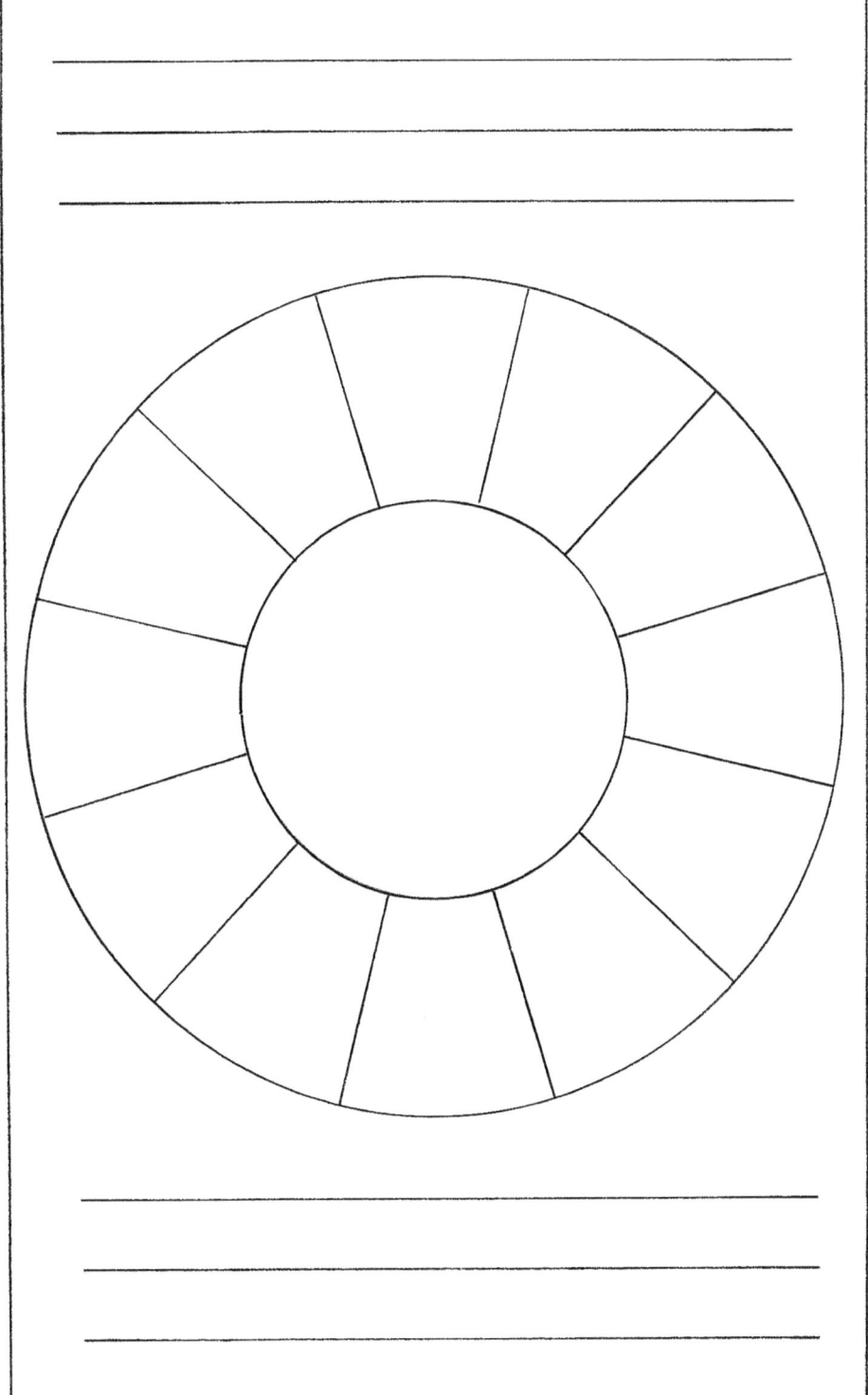

Template 11 2 rows of 36 spaces

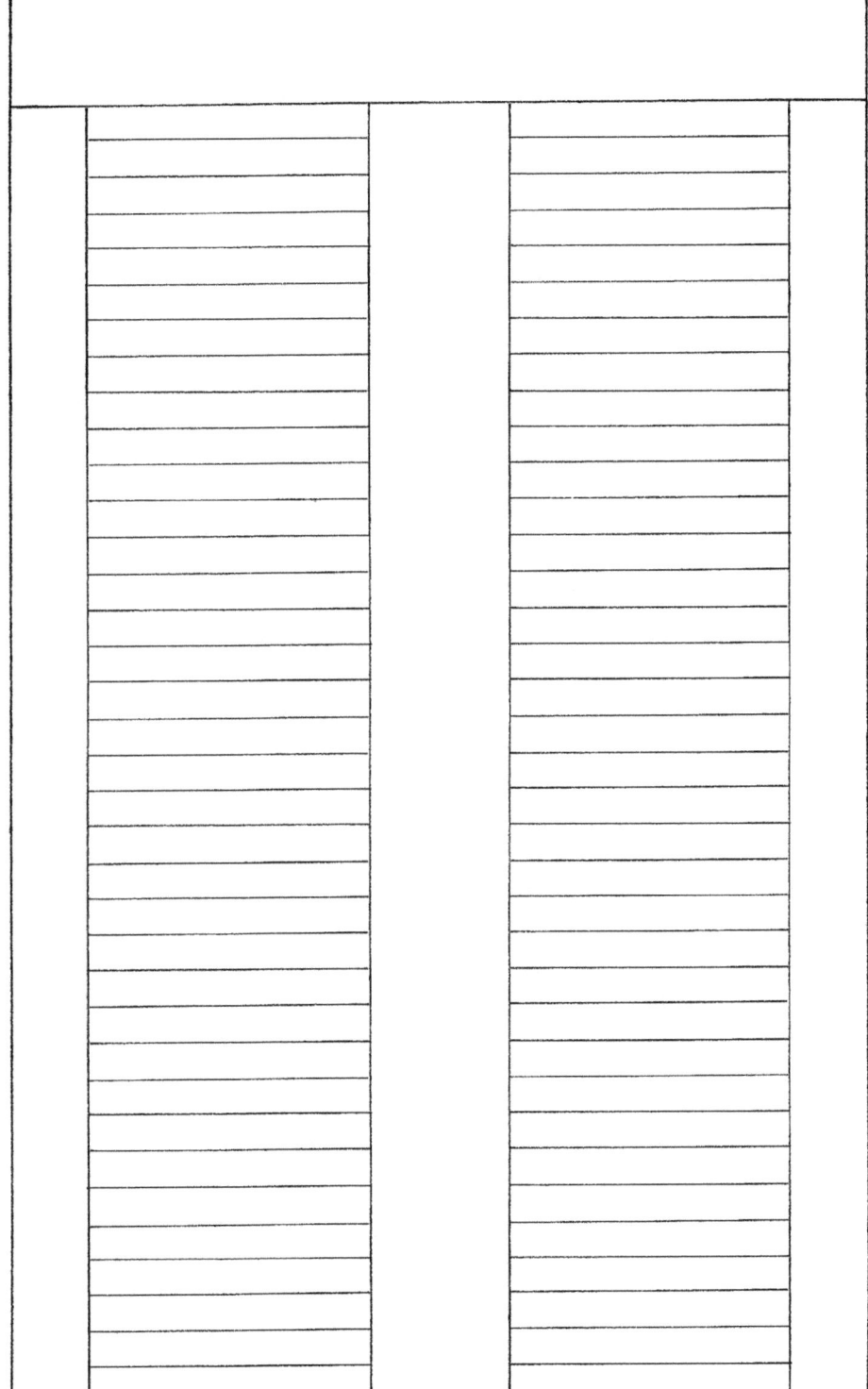

# Template 12 24 circles

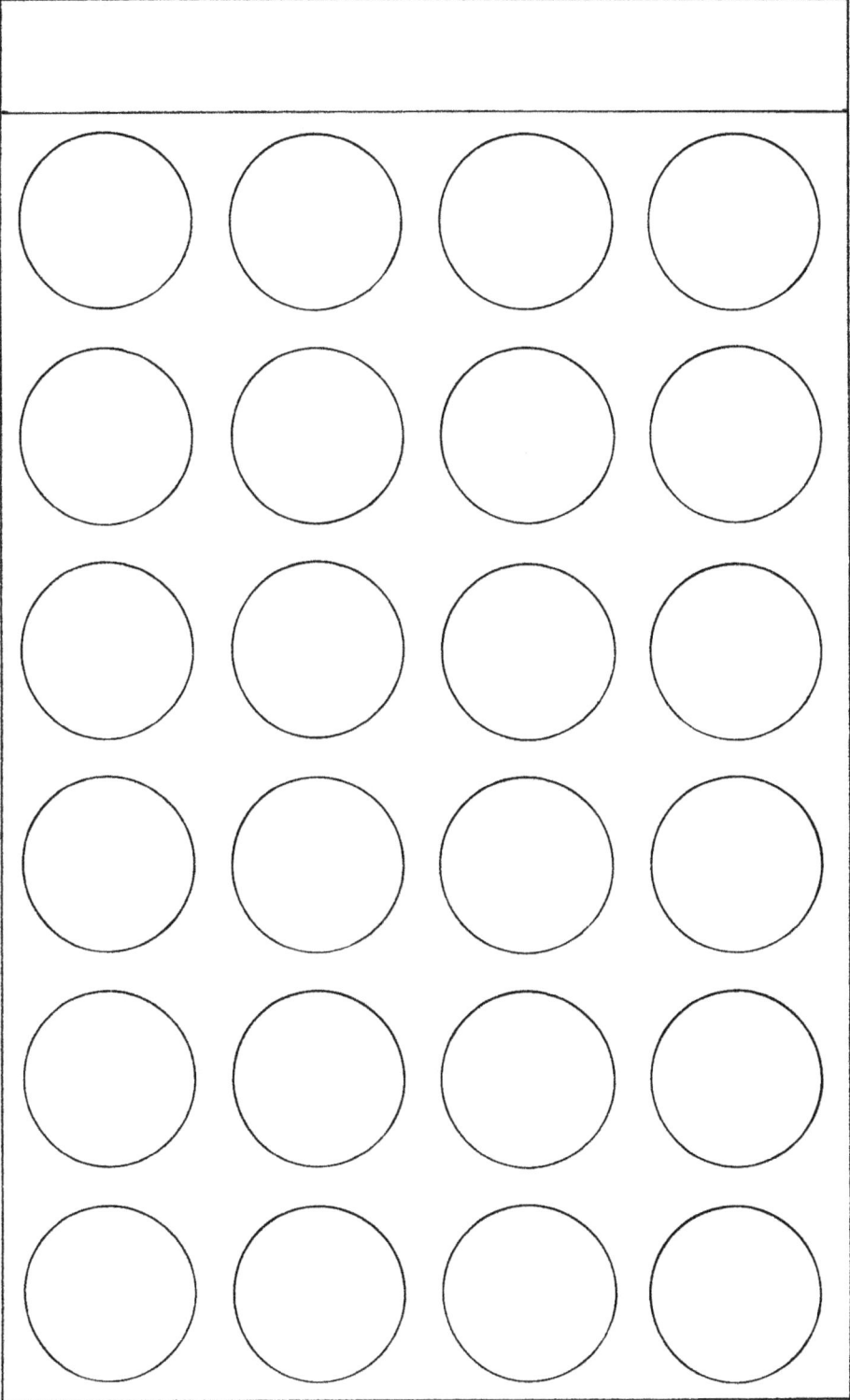

# Template 13  9 lines of 12 squares

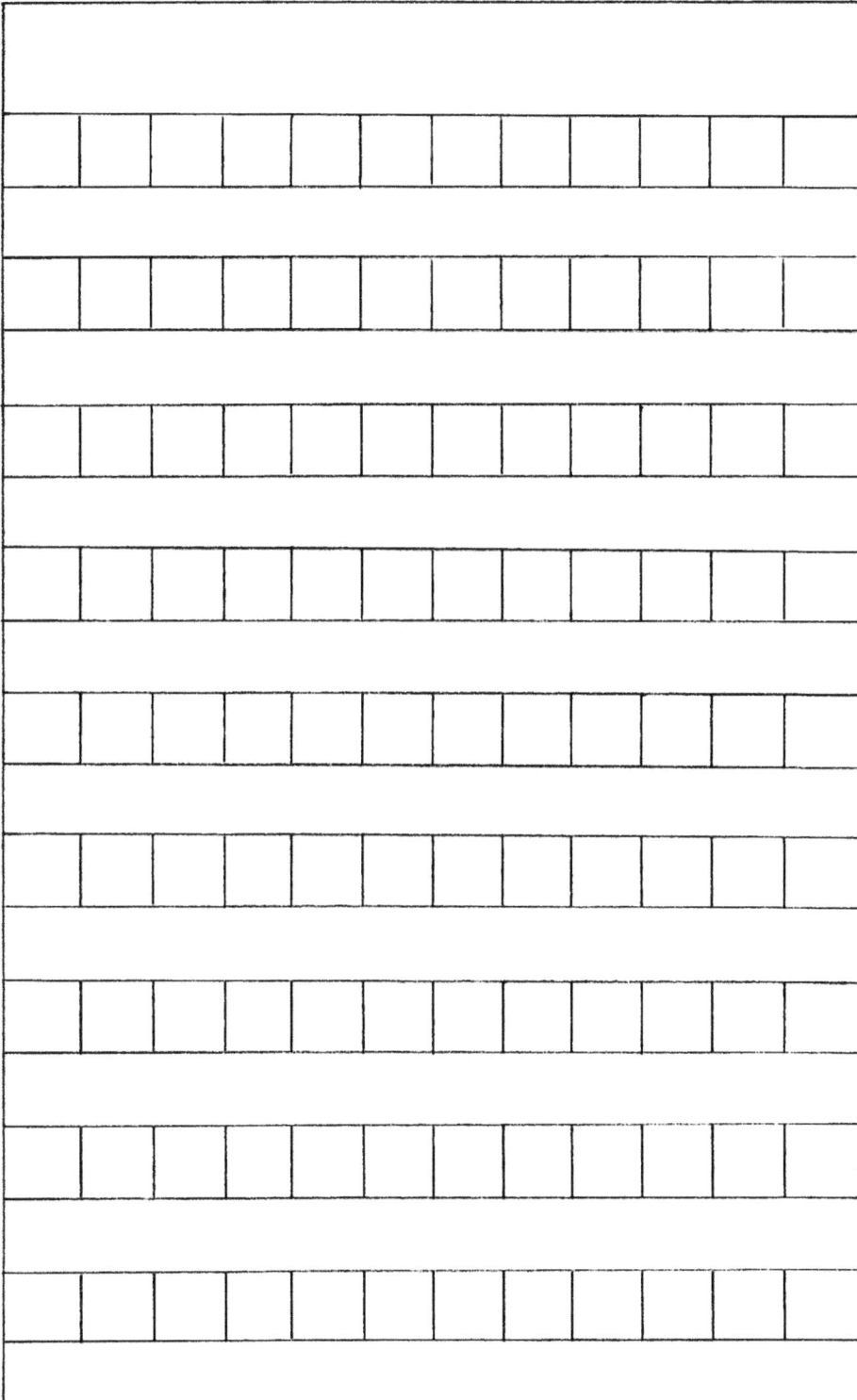

Template 14  36 spaces

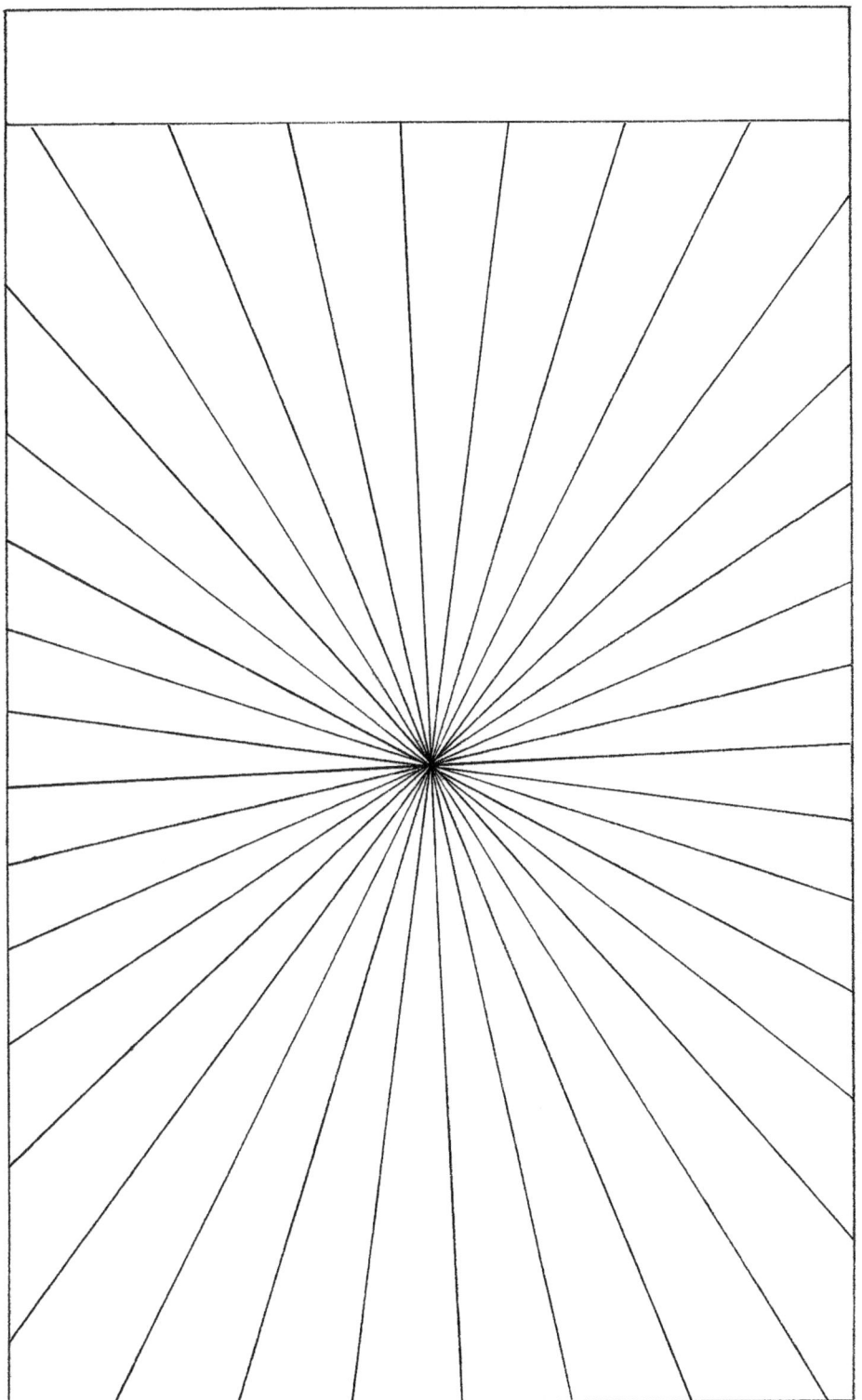

Template 15  1 bcolor Wheel of 36 spaces+ 4 quarters of 9 spaces

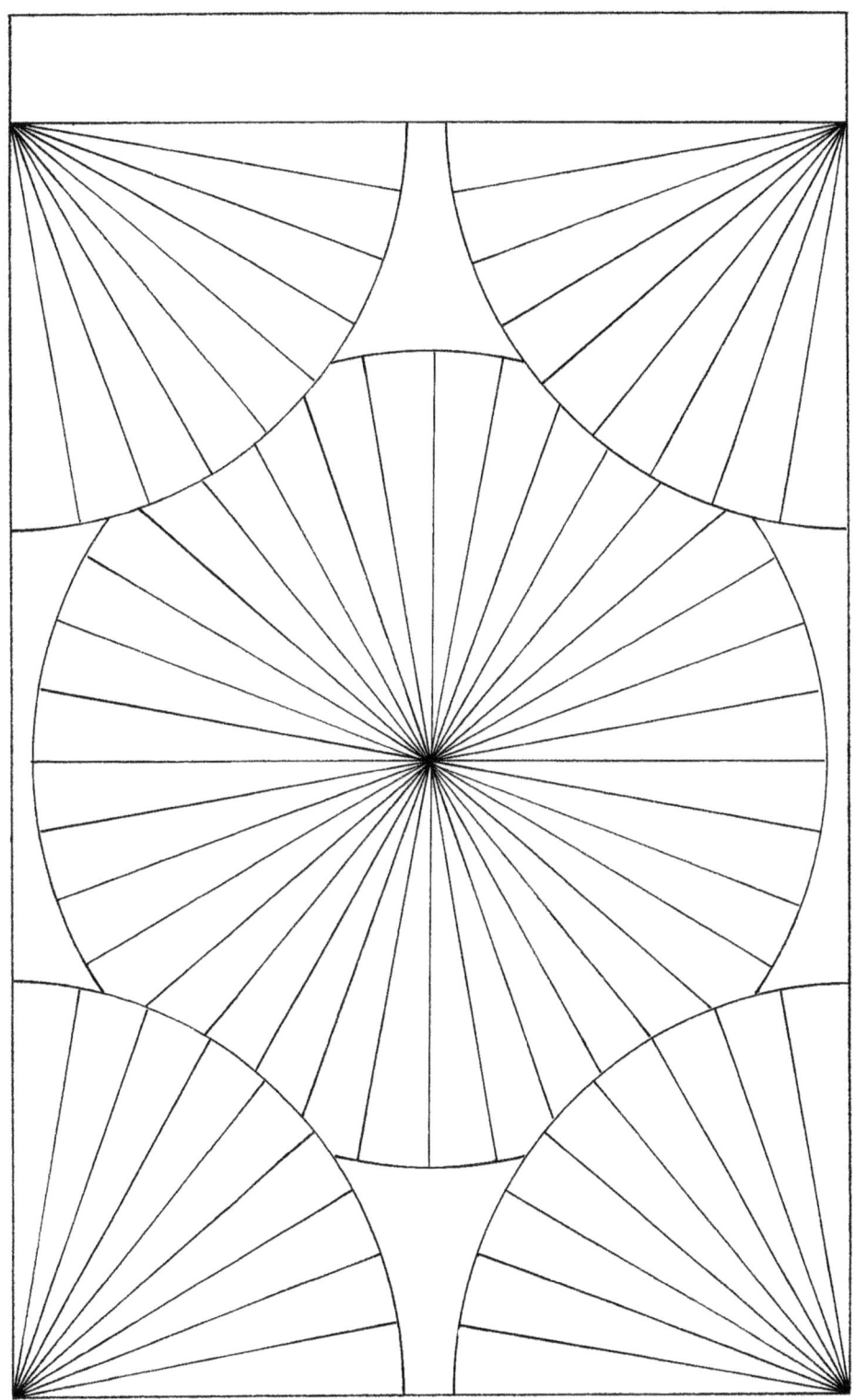

Template 1 Big Color Wheel 2x 72 spaces

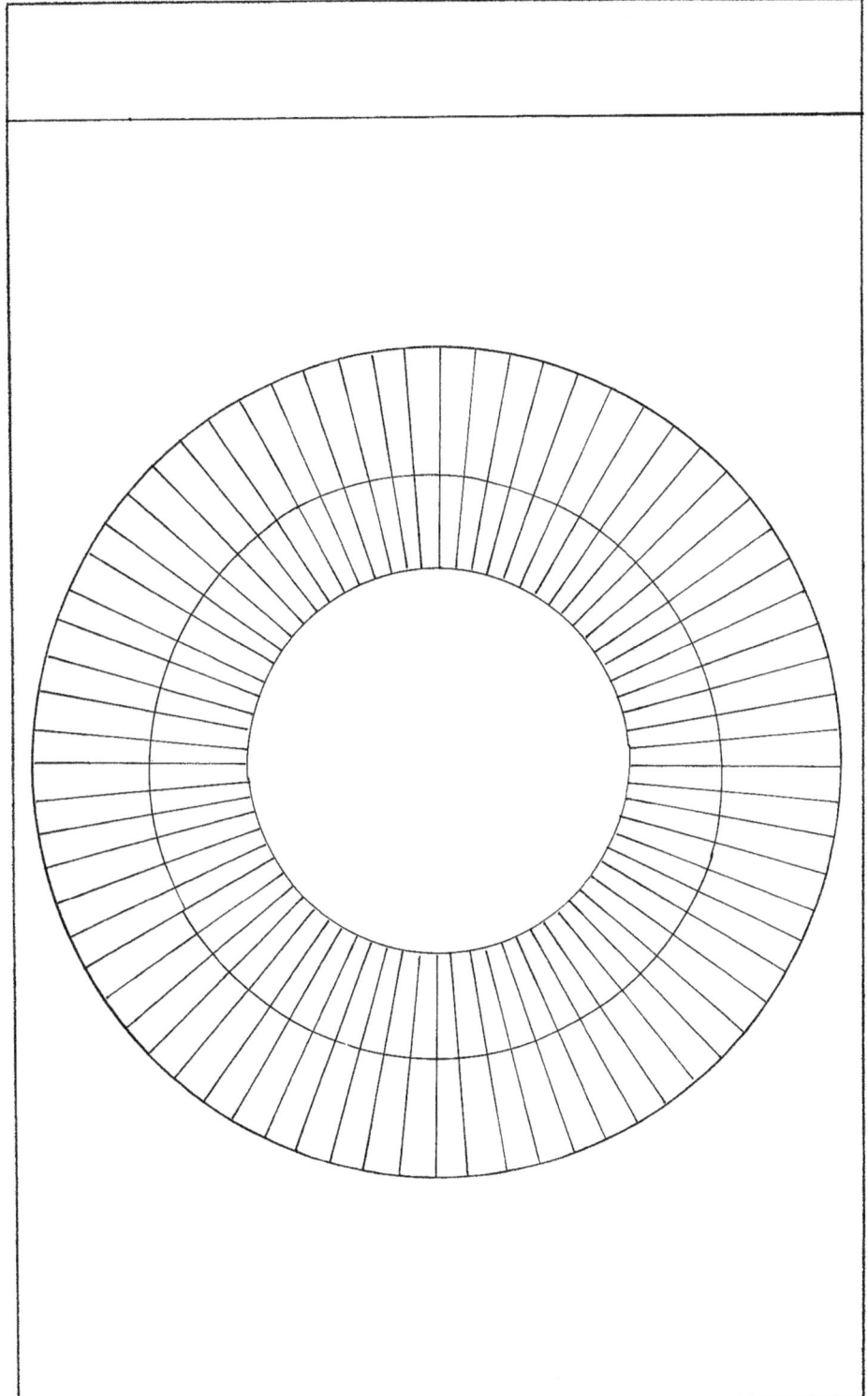

Template 2 Big Color Wheel 36 spaces

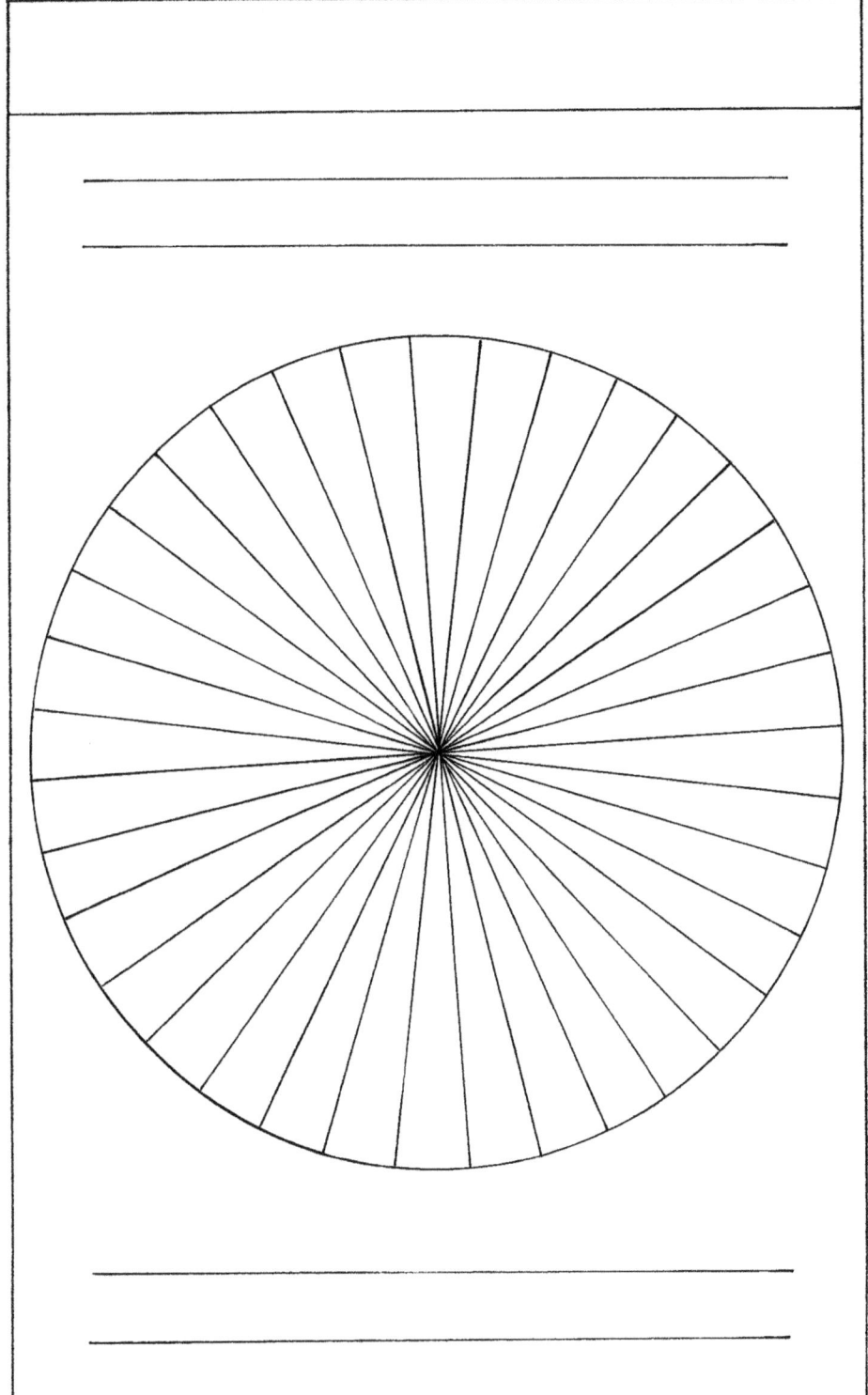

# Template 3 Big Color Wheel 2x18 spaces

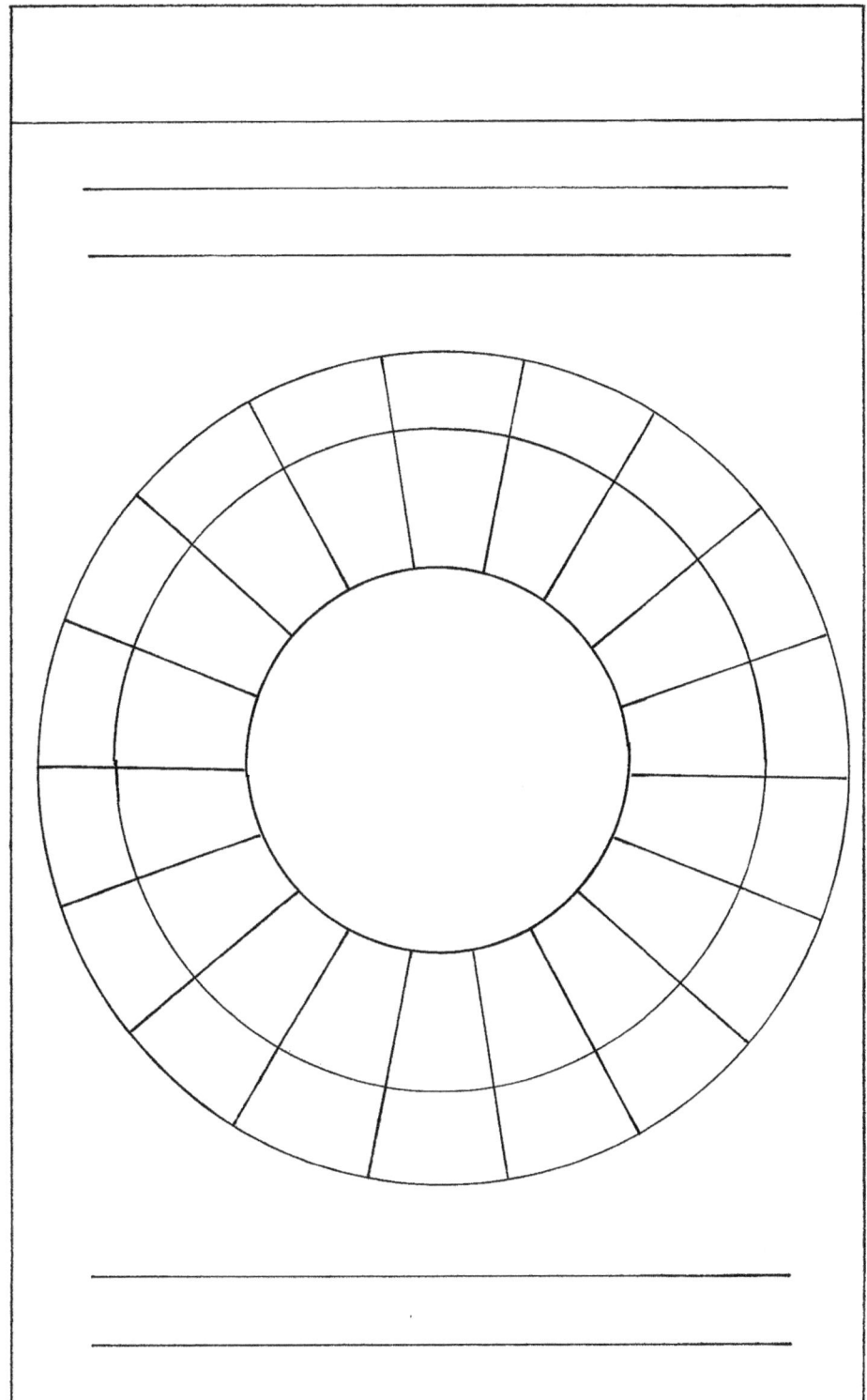

Template 4 Big Color Wheel 36 spaces

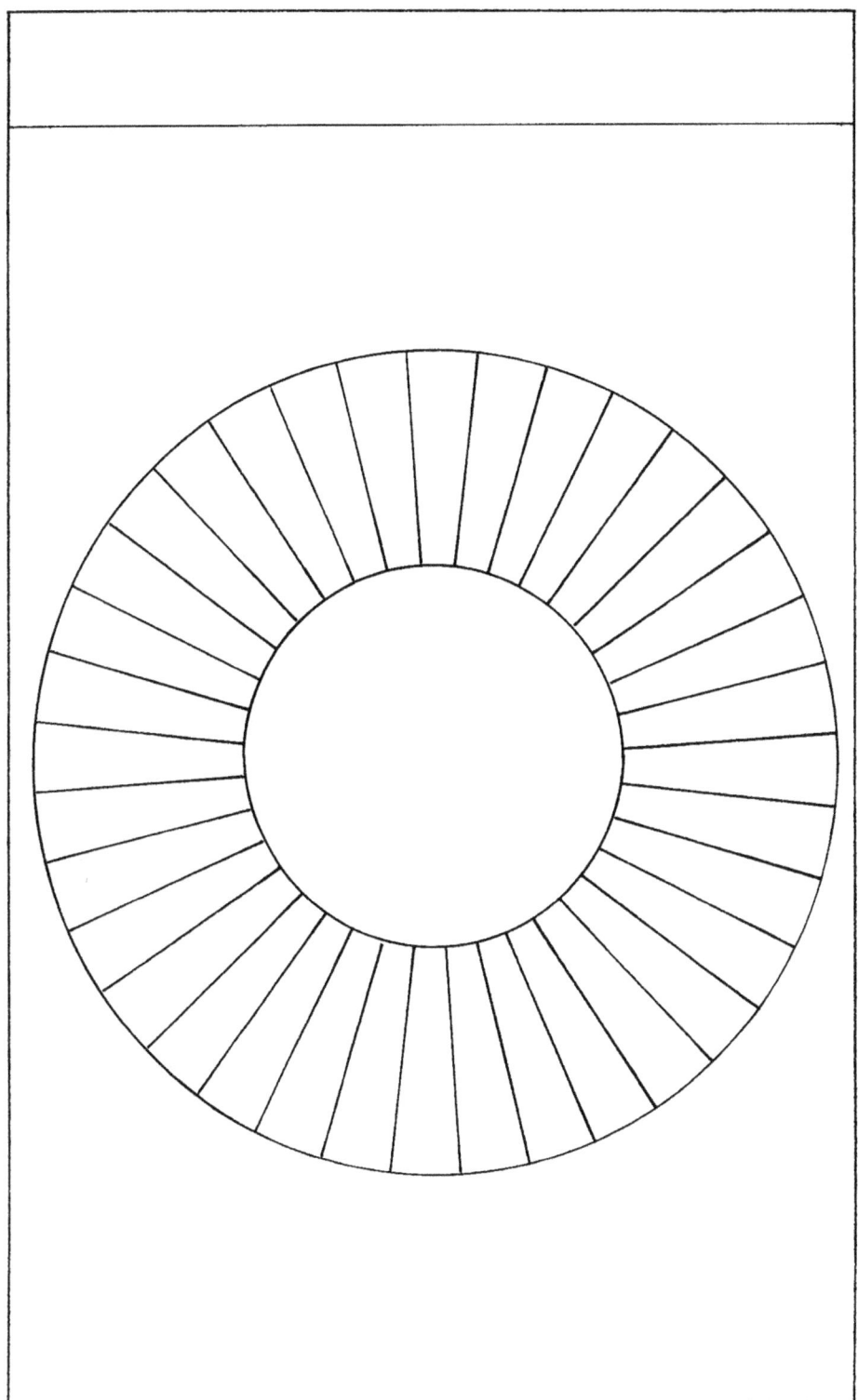

Template 5 15 blogs of 6 spaces

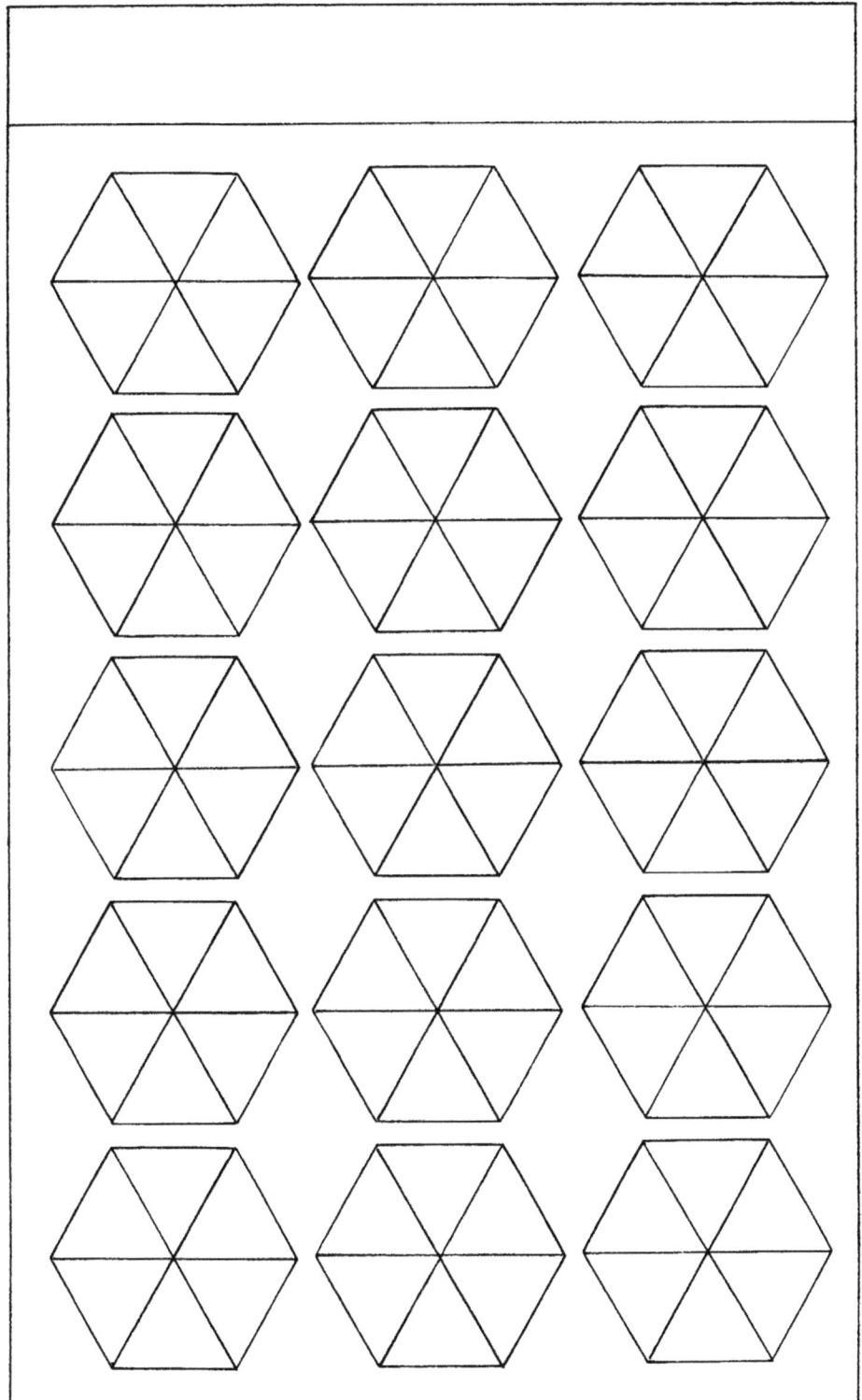

Template 6 6 squares of 4x6 spaces

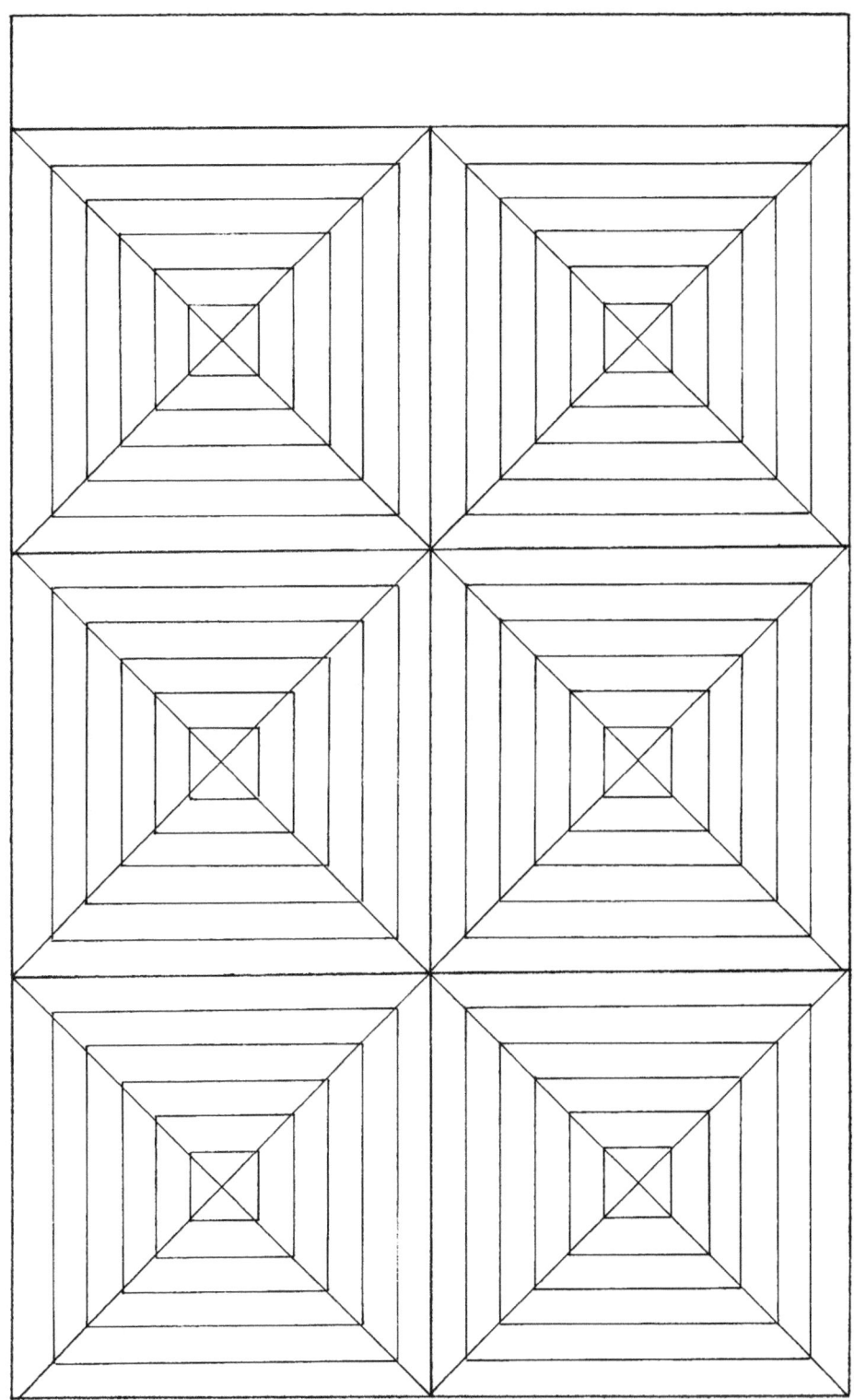

# Template 7 endless possibilities

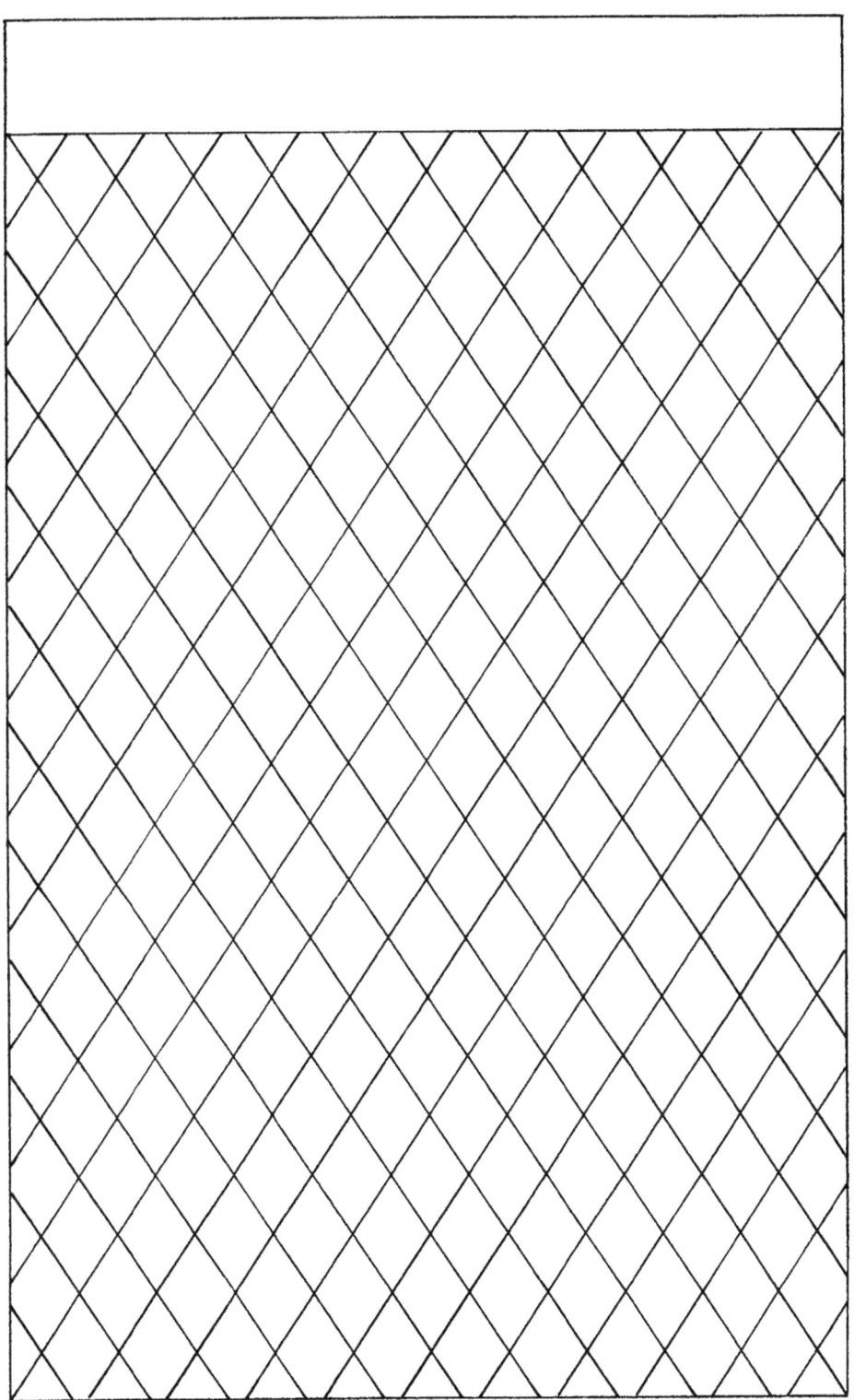

Template 8 6 lines of 32 spaces

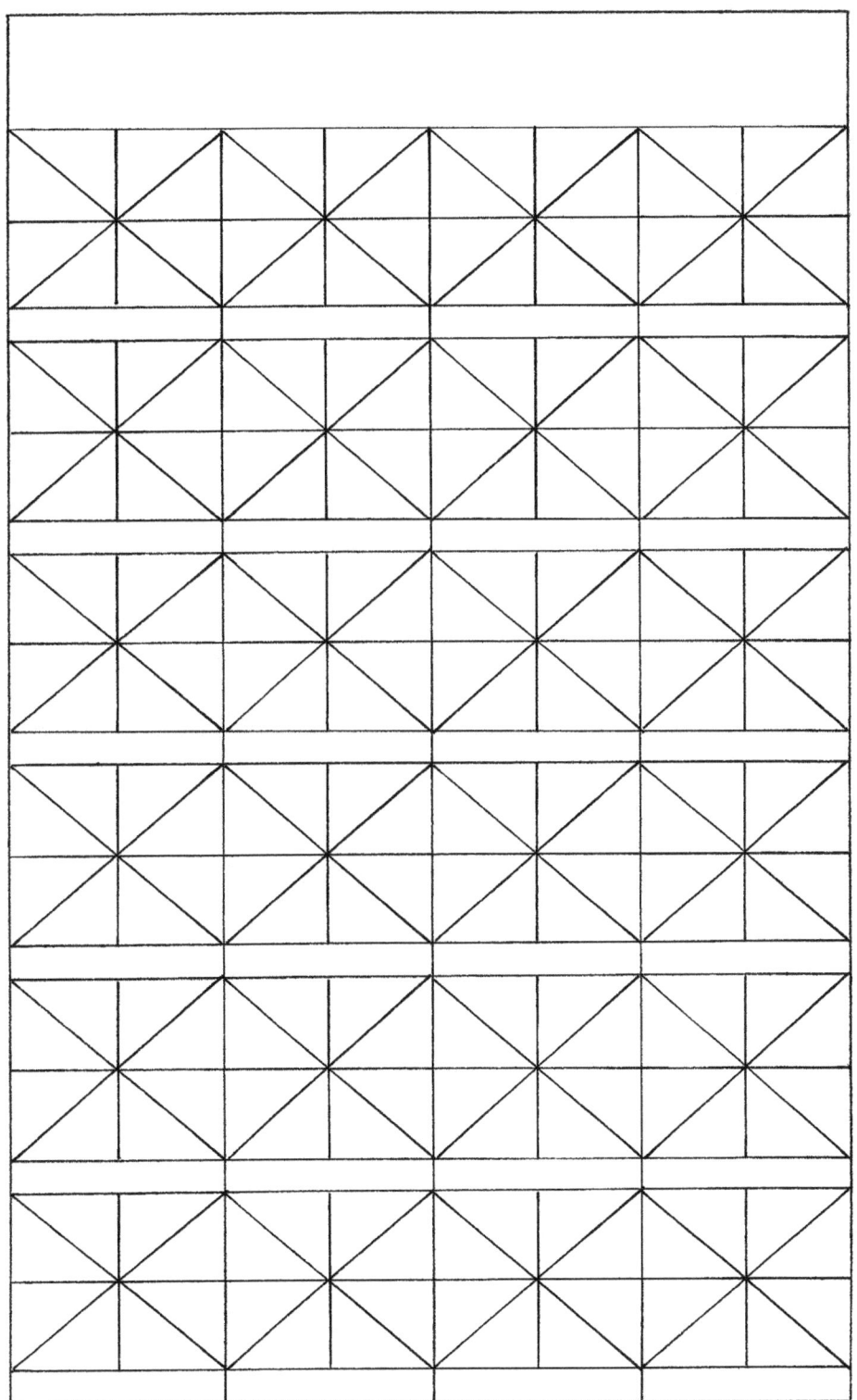

Template 9 6 lines of 24 spaces

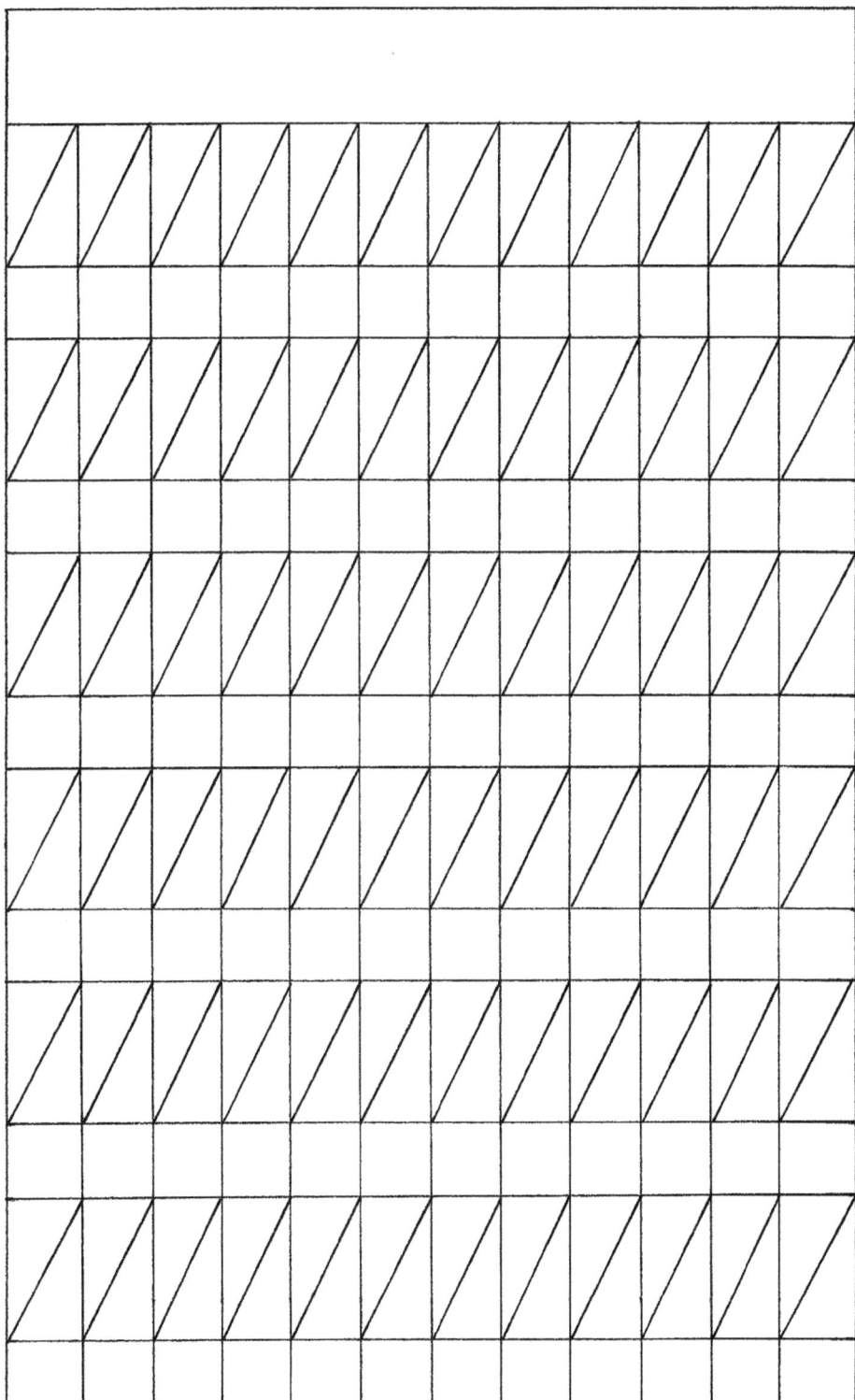

Template 10 Color Wheel 12 spaces

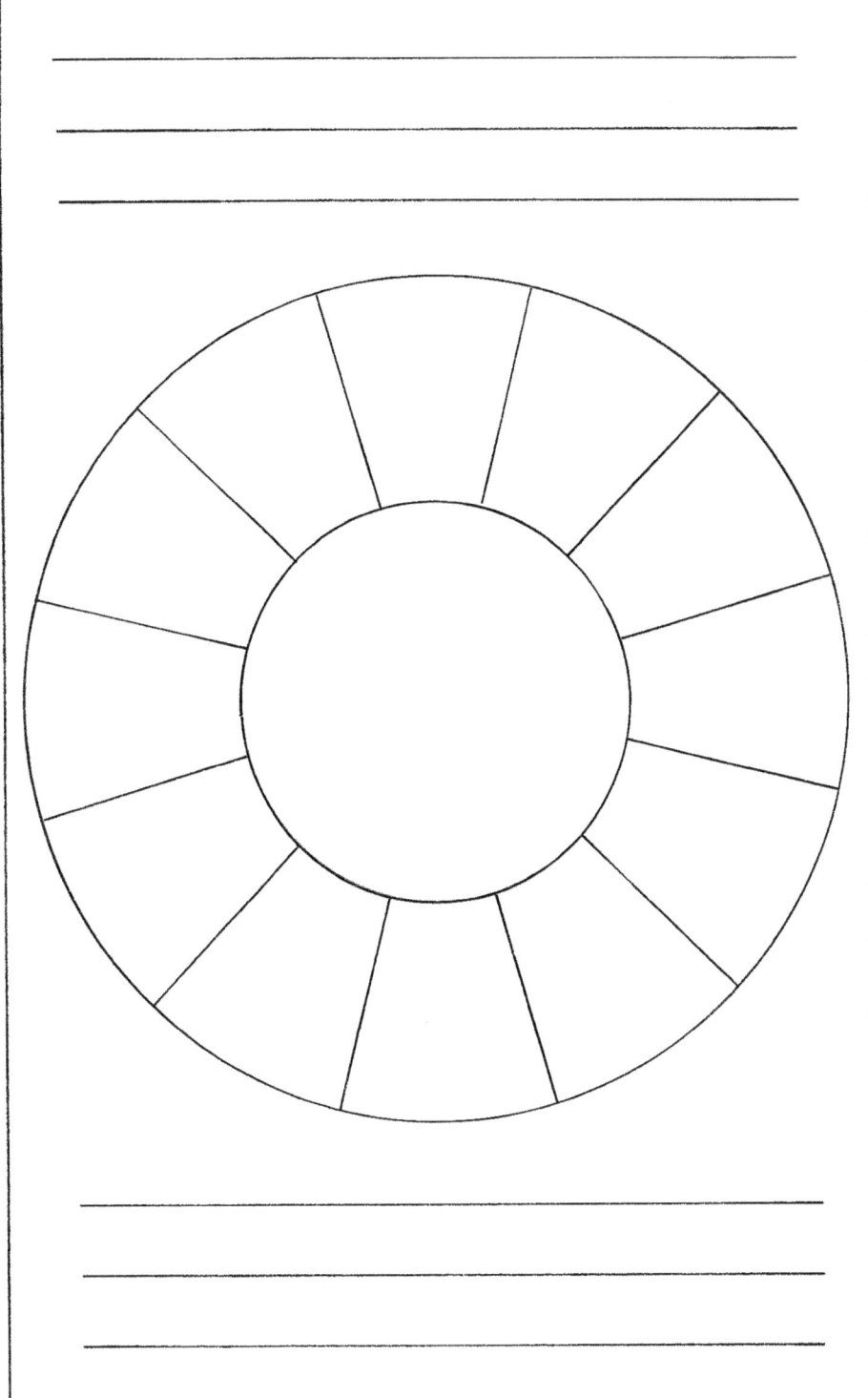

Template 11 2 rows of 36 spaces

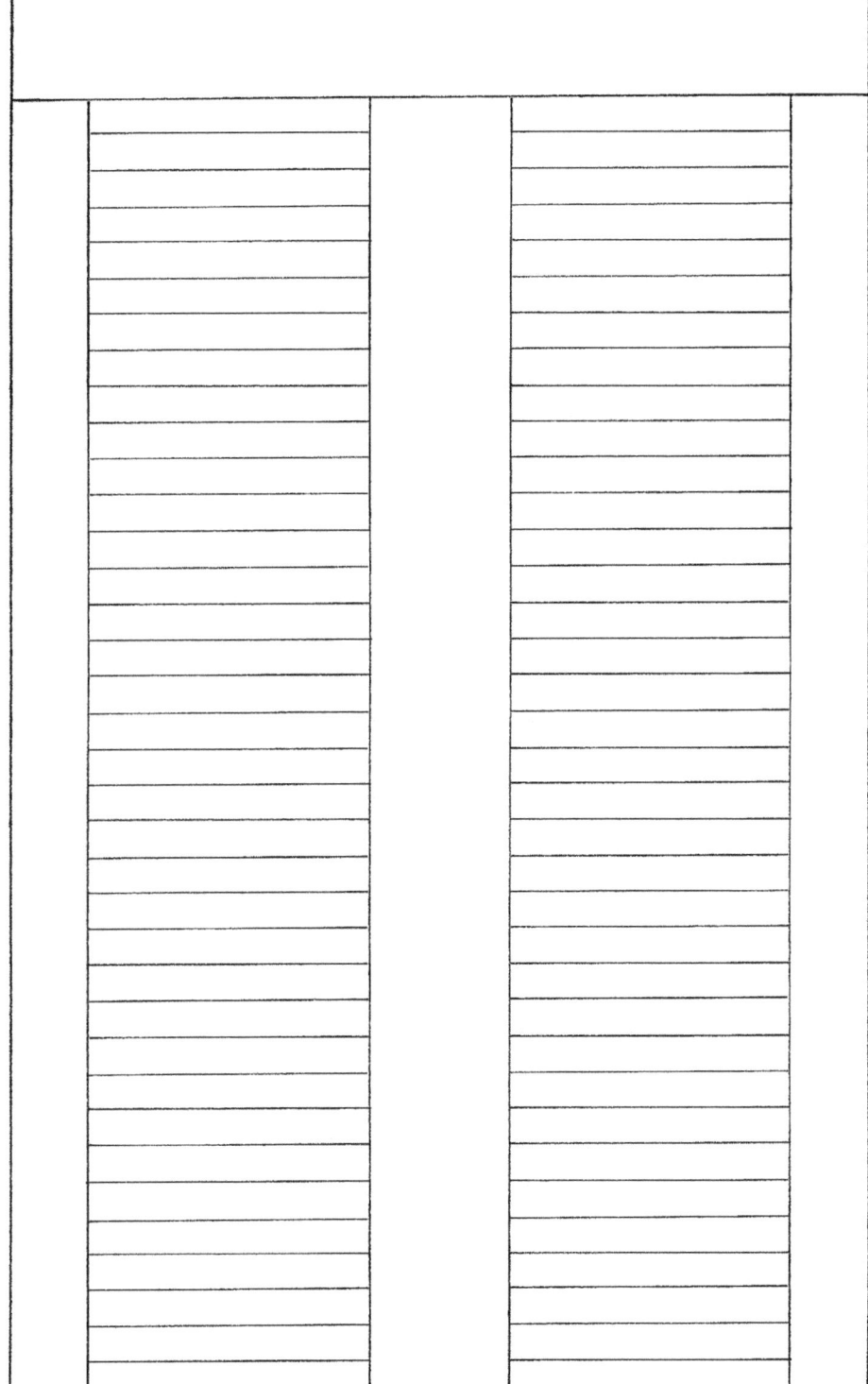

# Template 12 24 circles

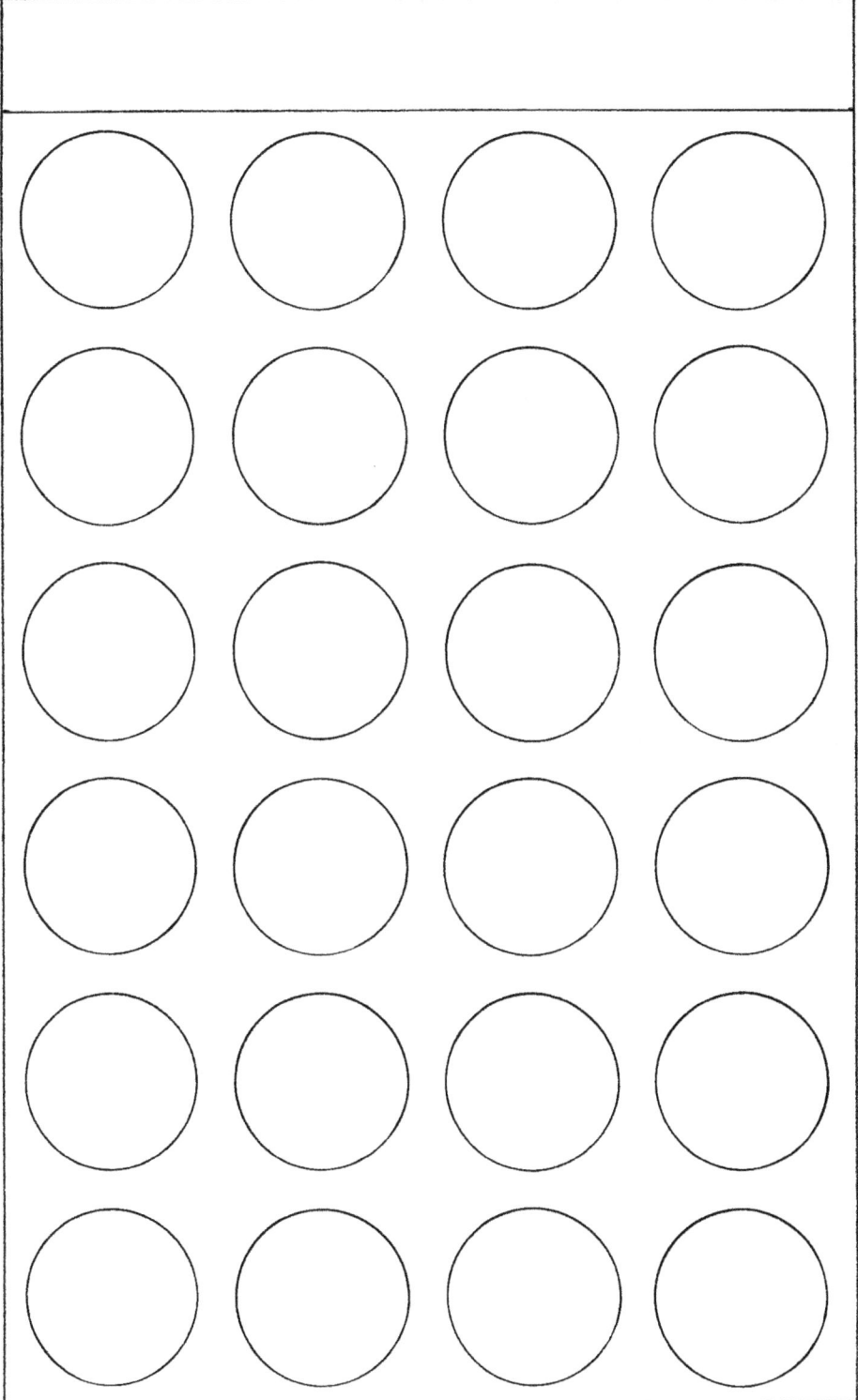

Template 13  9 lines of 12 squares

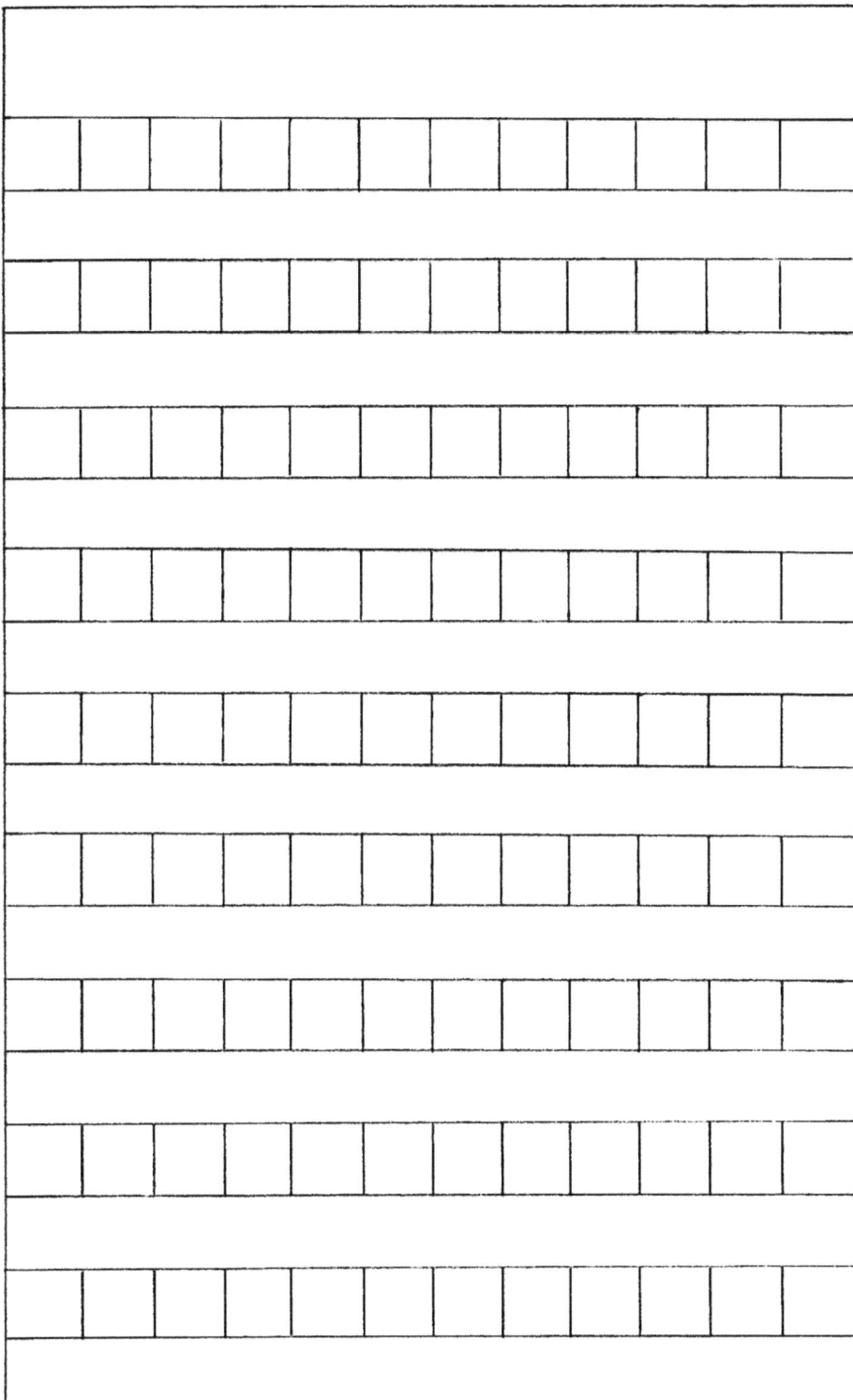

Template 14  36 spaces

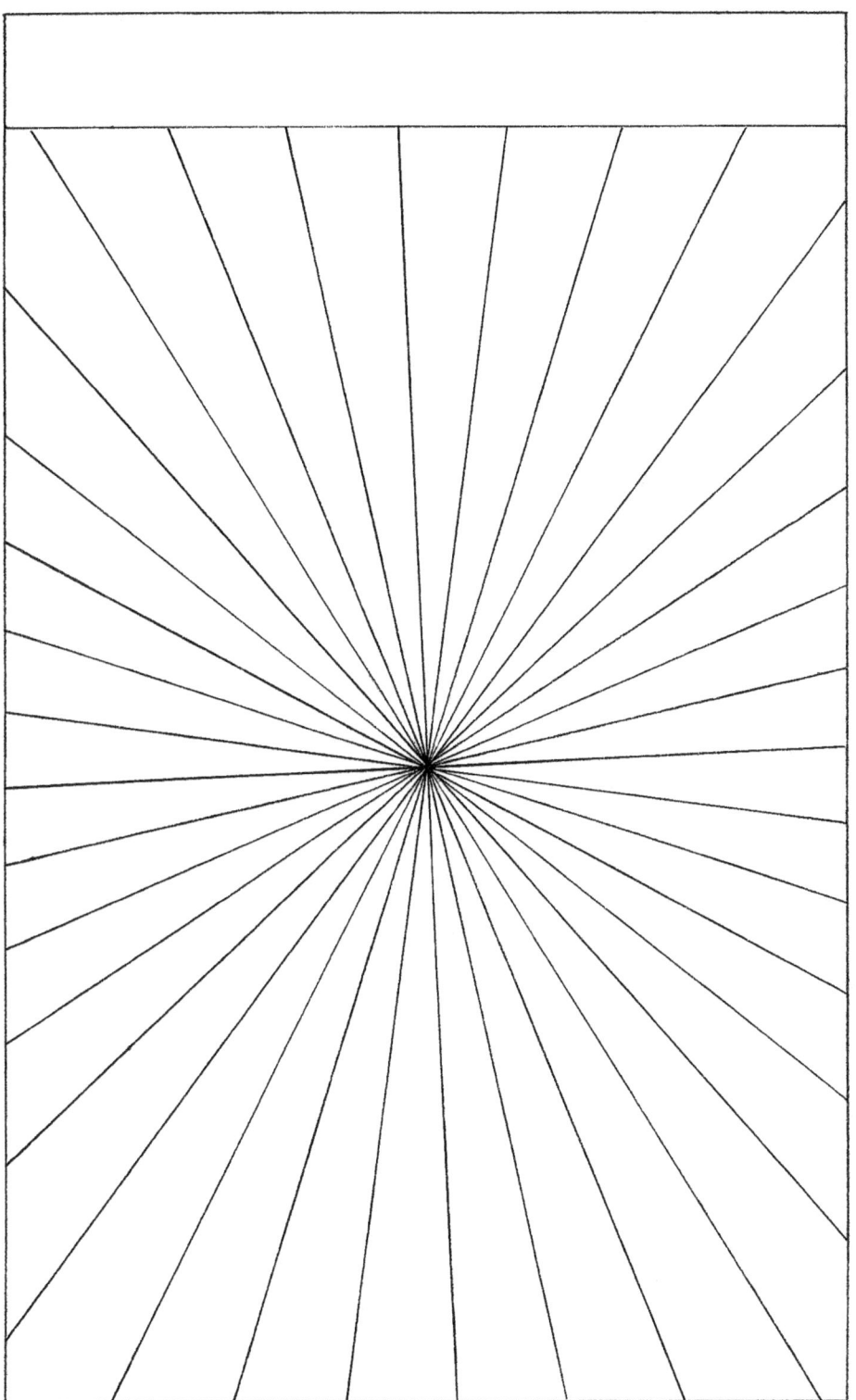

Template 15  1 bcolor Wheel of 36 spaces+ 4 quarters of 9 spaces

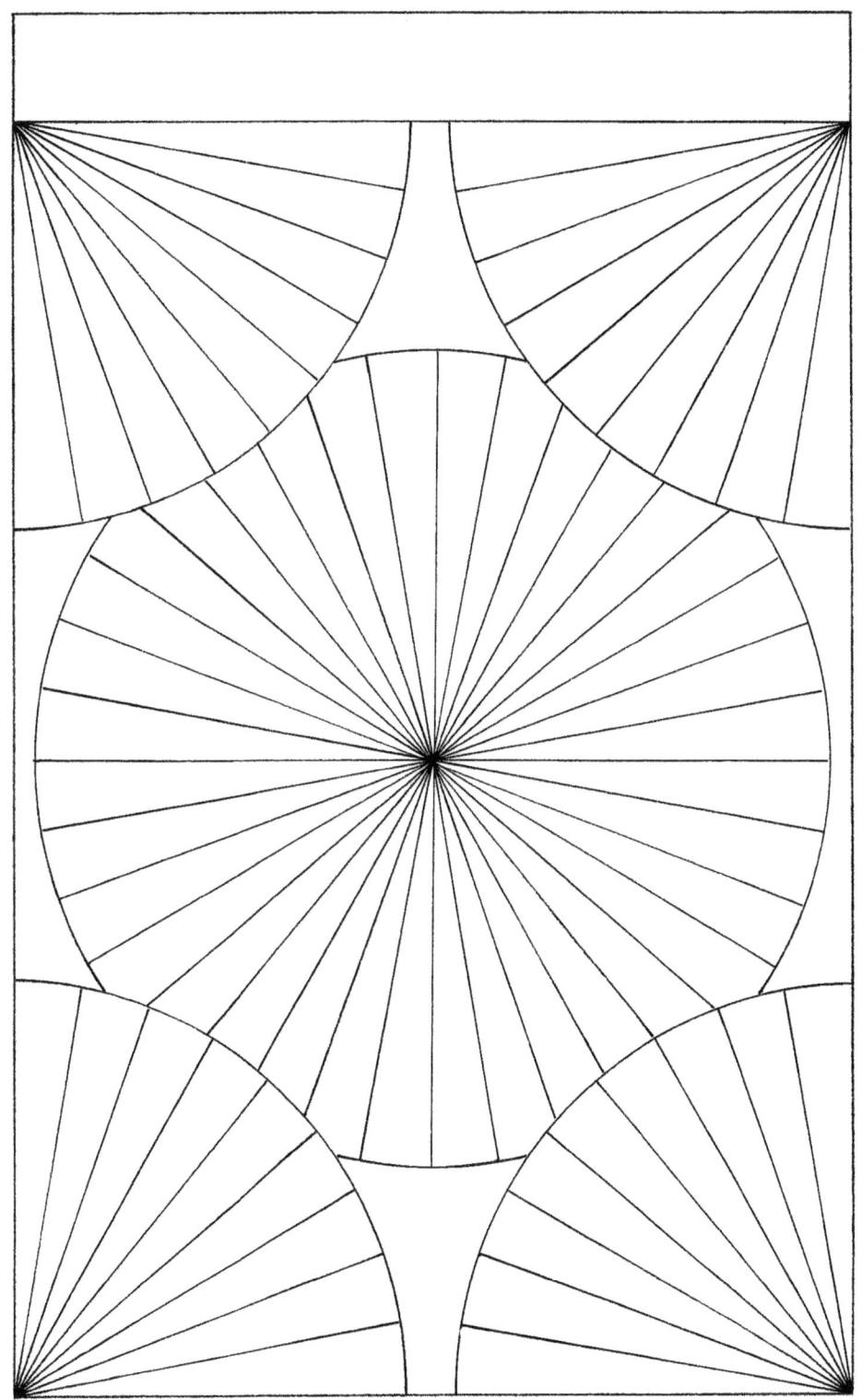

Template 1 Big Color Wheel 2x 72 spaces

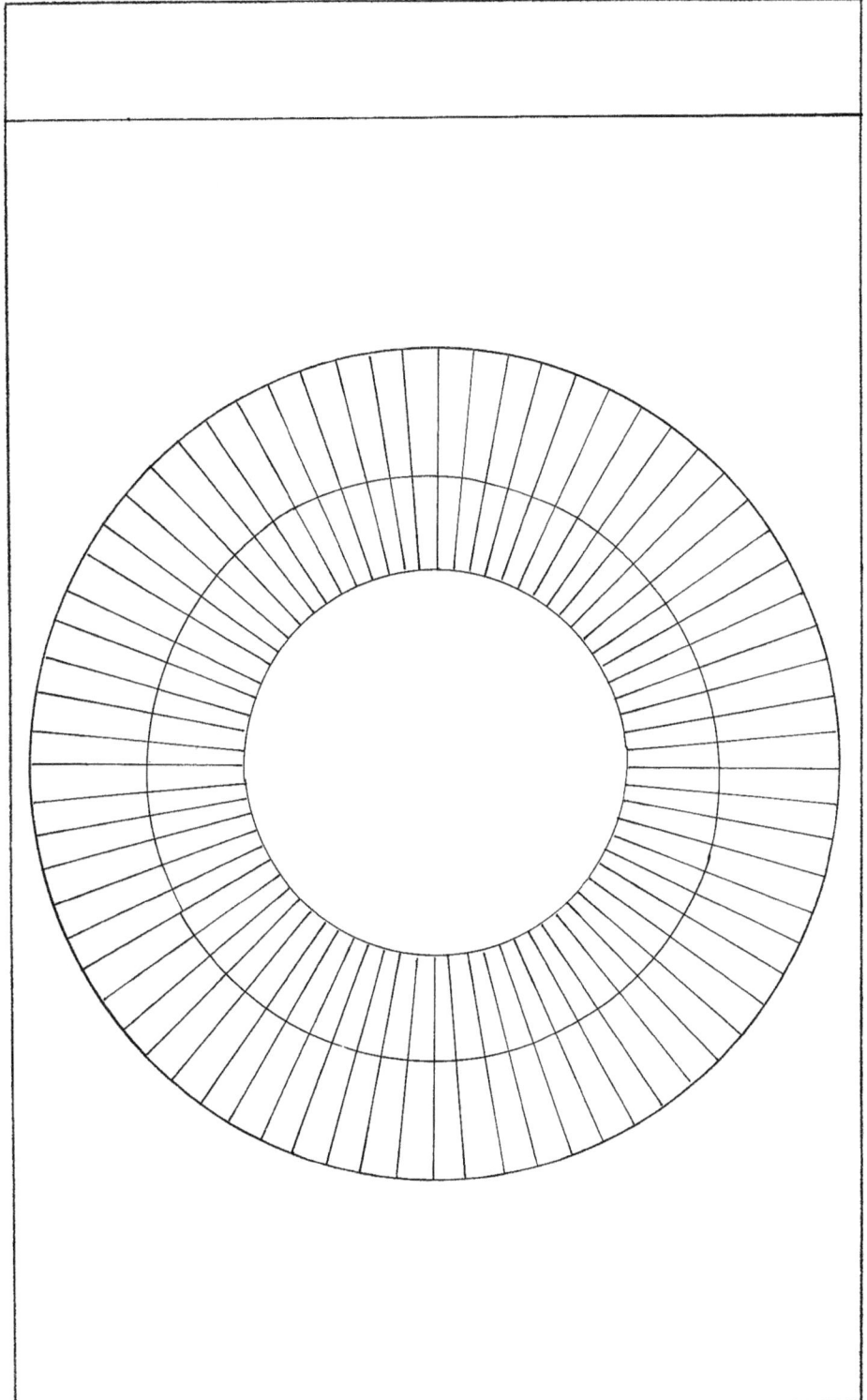

Template 2 Big Color Wheel 36 spaces

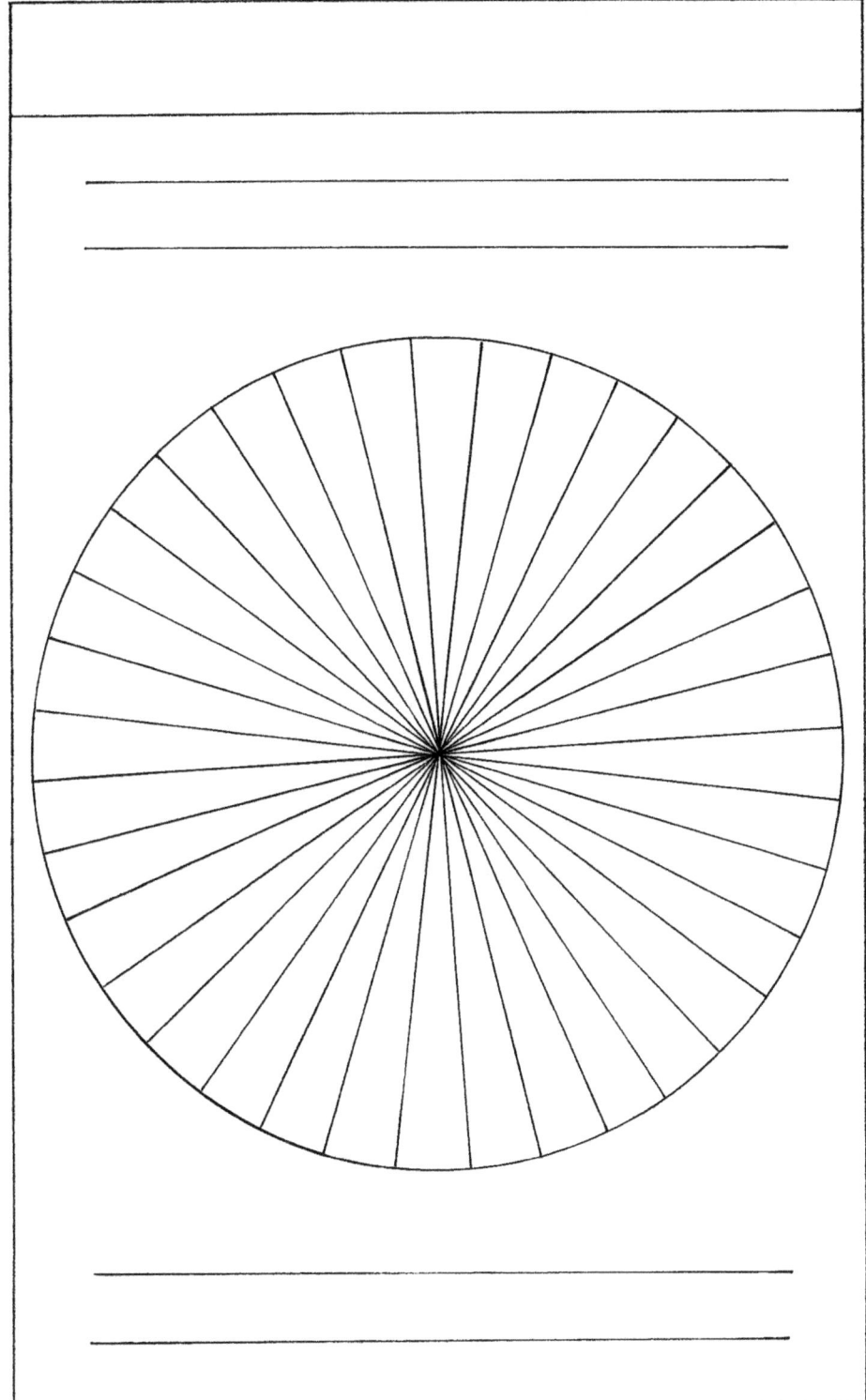

Template 3 Big Color Wheel 2x18 spaces

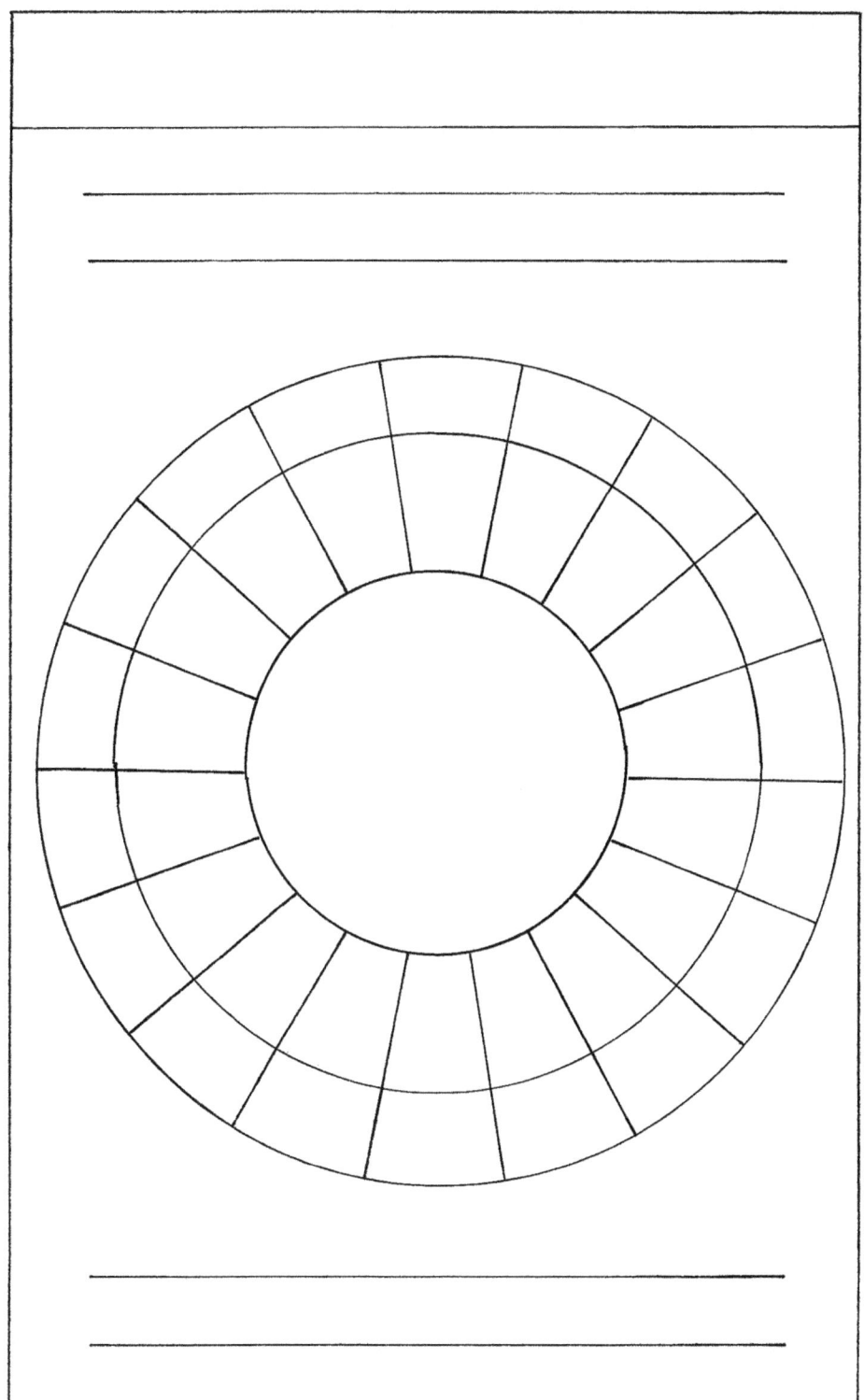

Template 4 Big Color Wheel 36 spaces

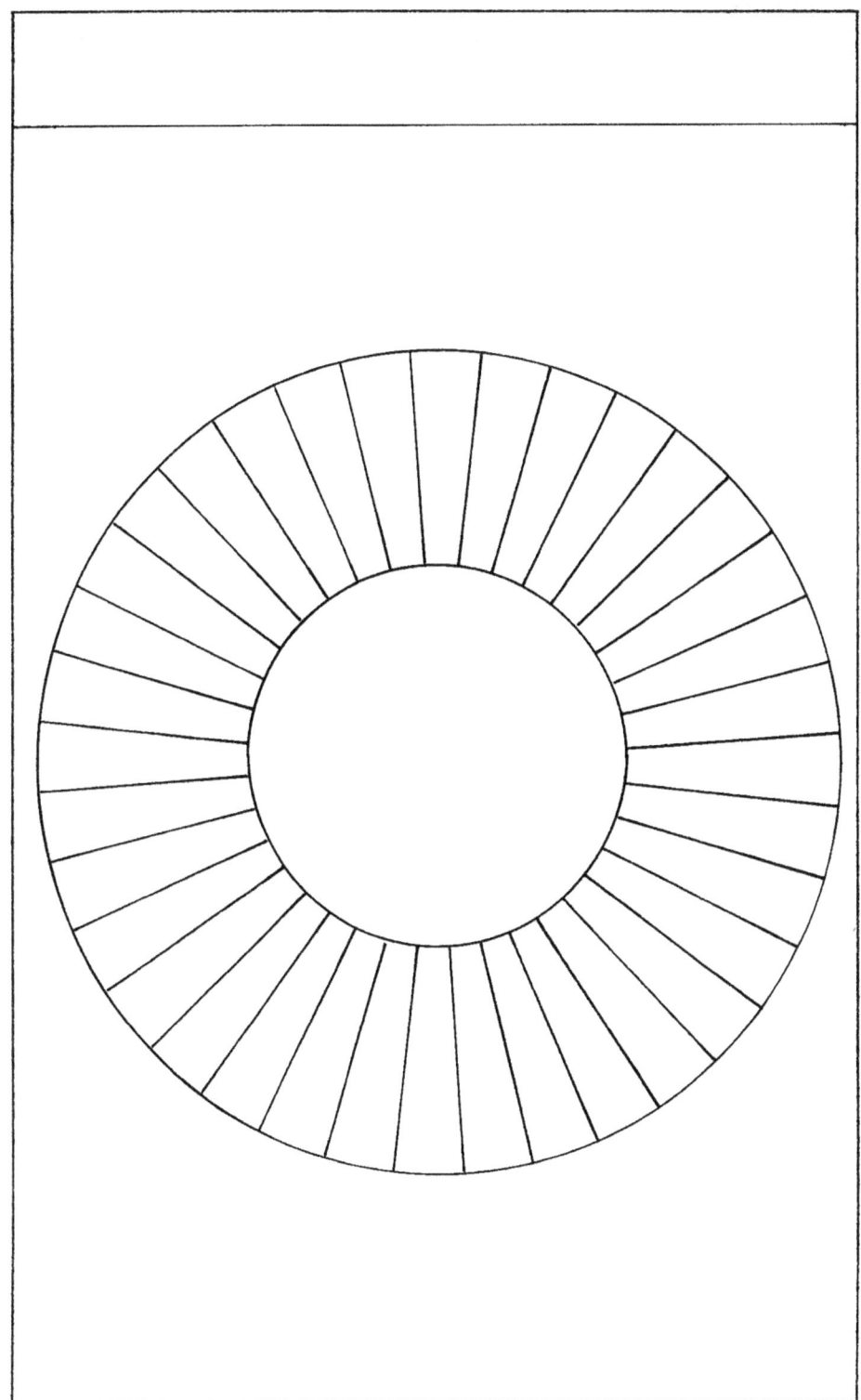

# Template 5 15 blogs of 6 spaces

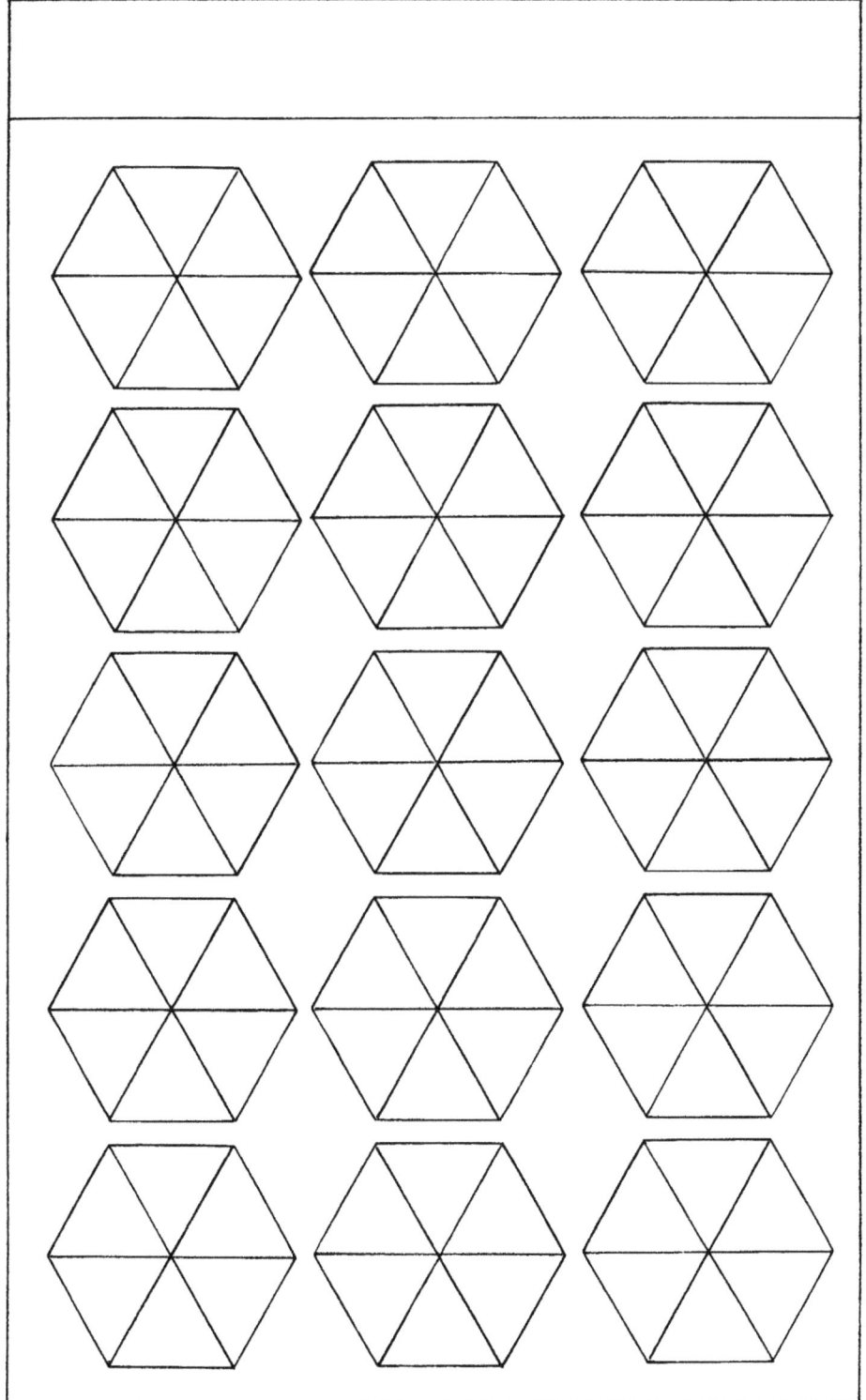

# Template 6 6 squares of 4x6 spaces

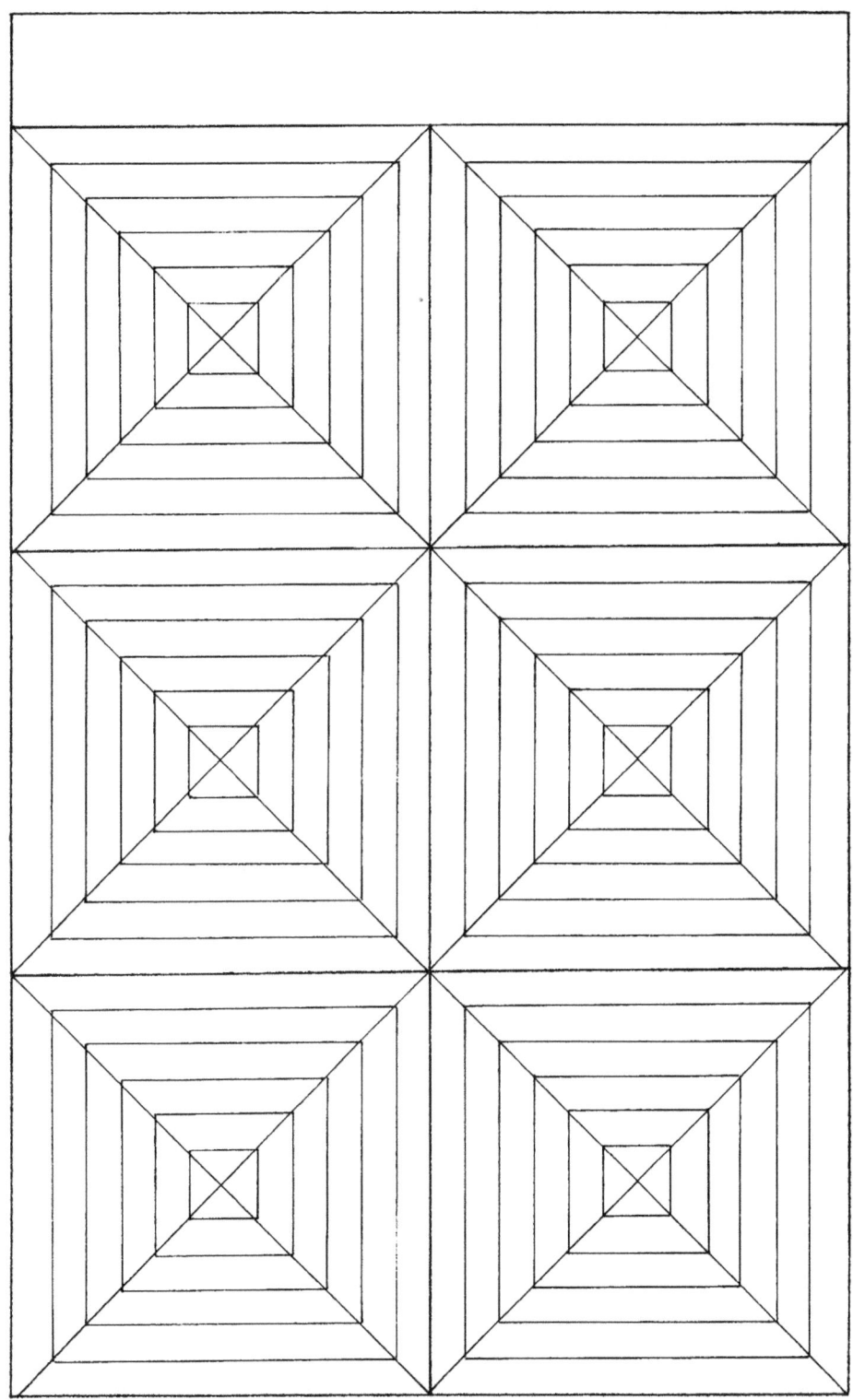

# Template 7 endless possibilities

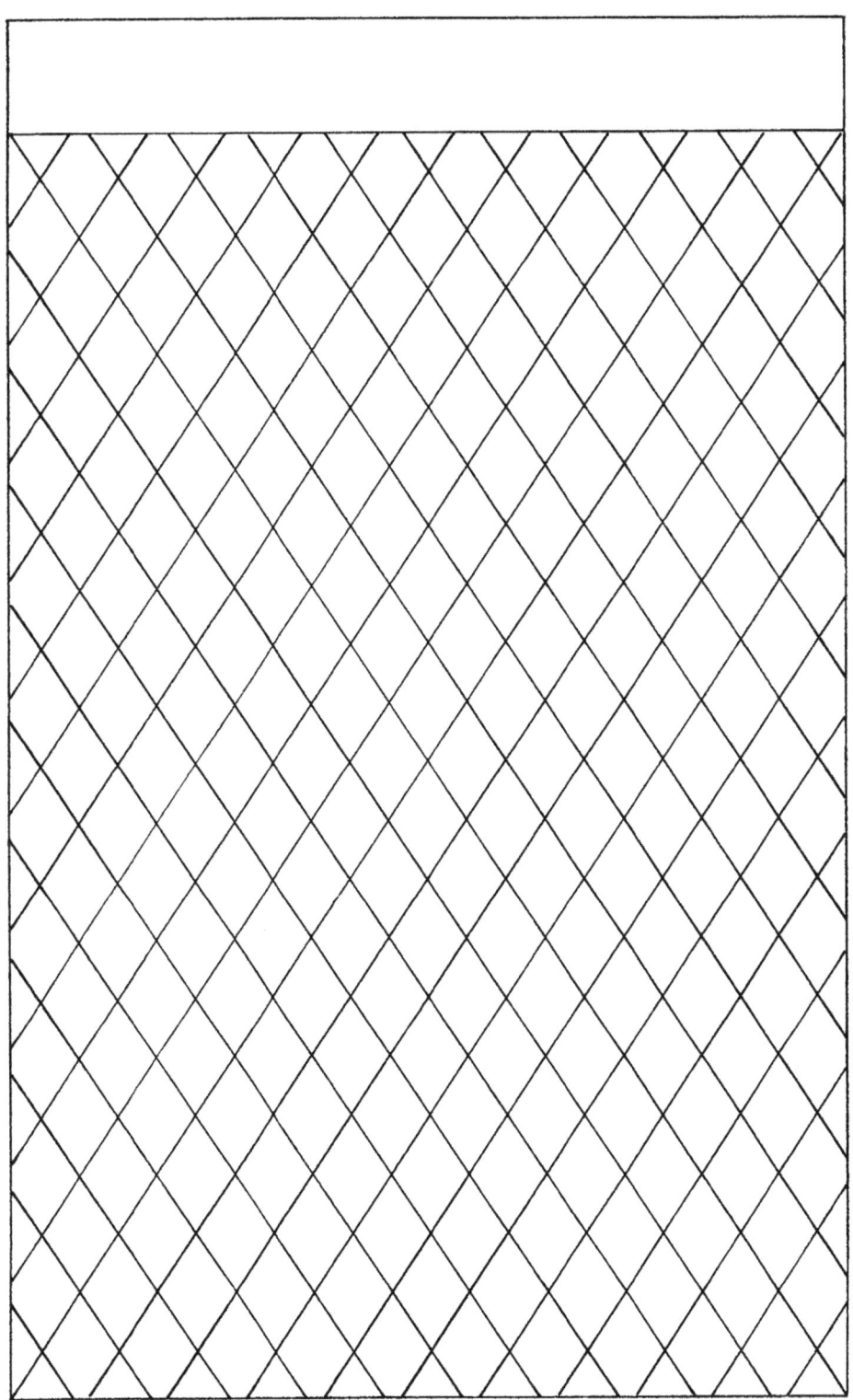

Template 8 6 lines of 32 spaces

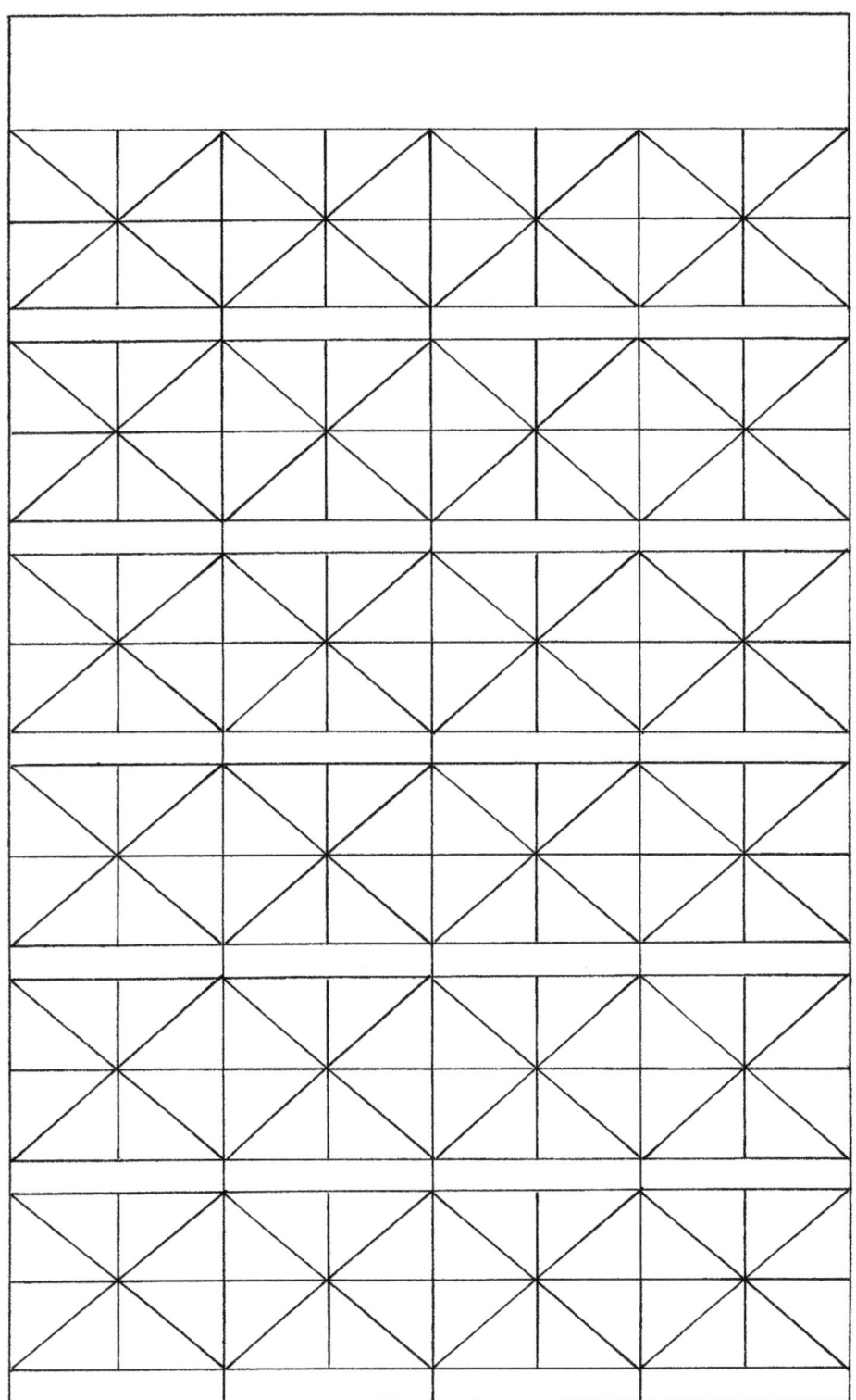

Template 9 6 lines of 24 spaces

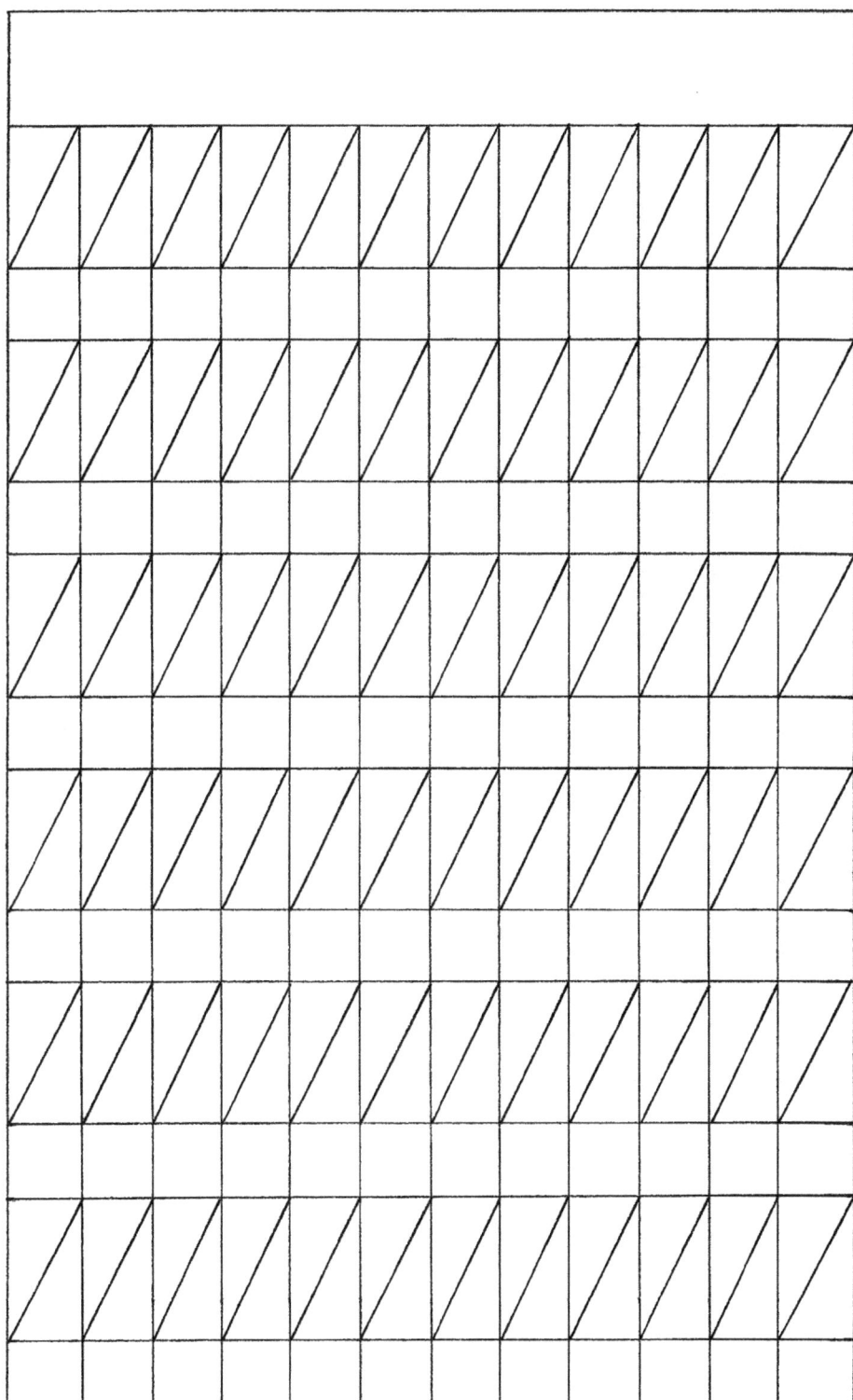

Template 10 Color Wheel 12 spaces

_____

_____

_____

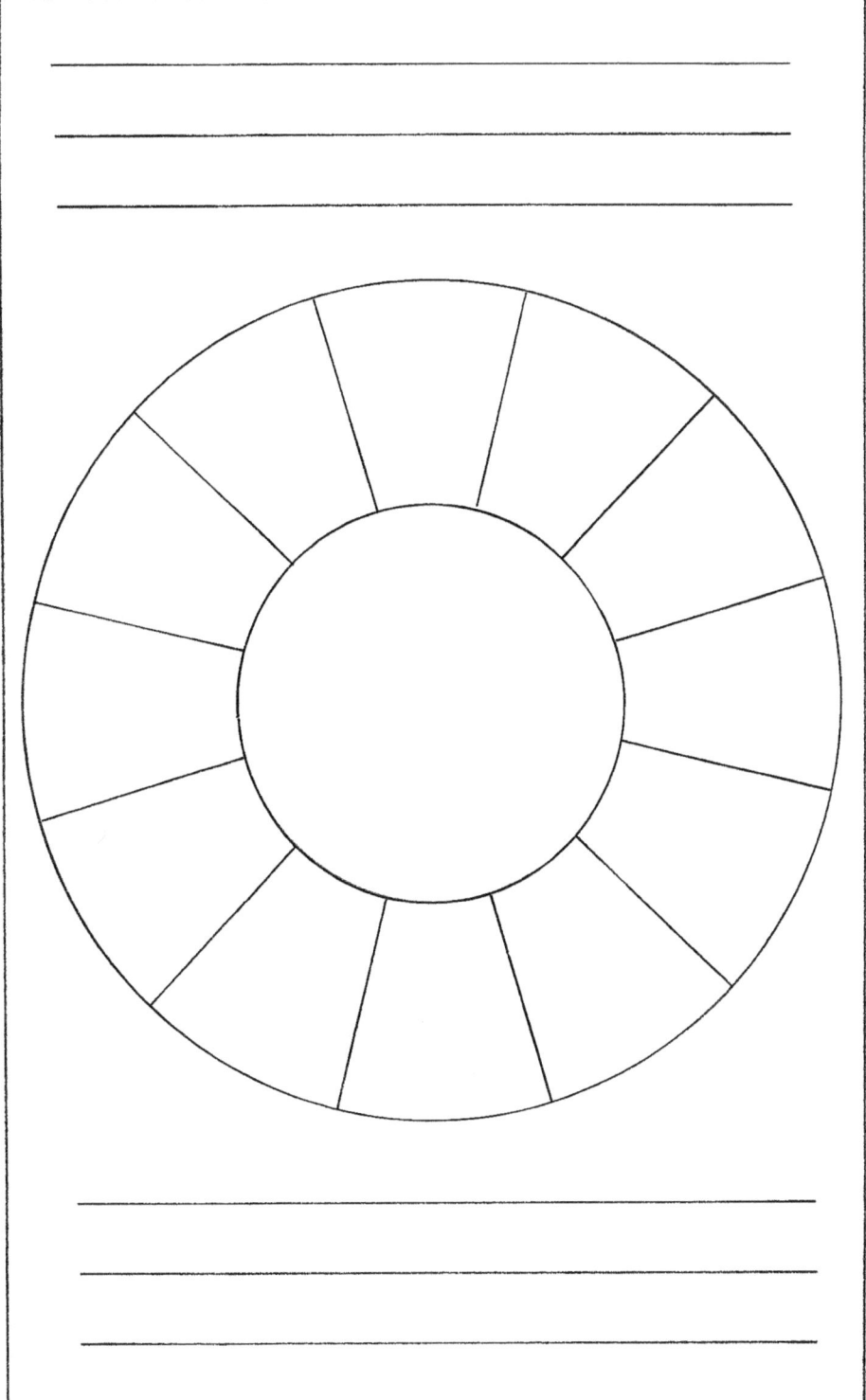

_____

_____

_____

Template 11 2 rows of 36 spaces

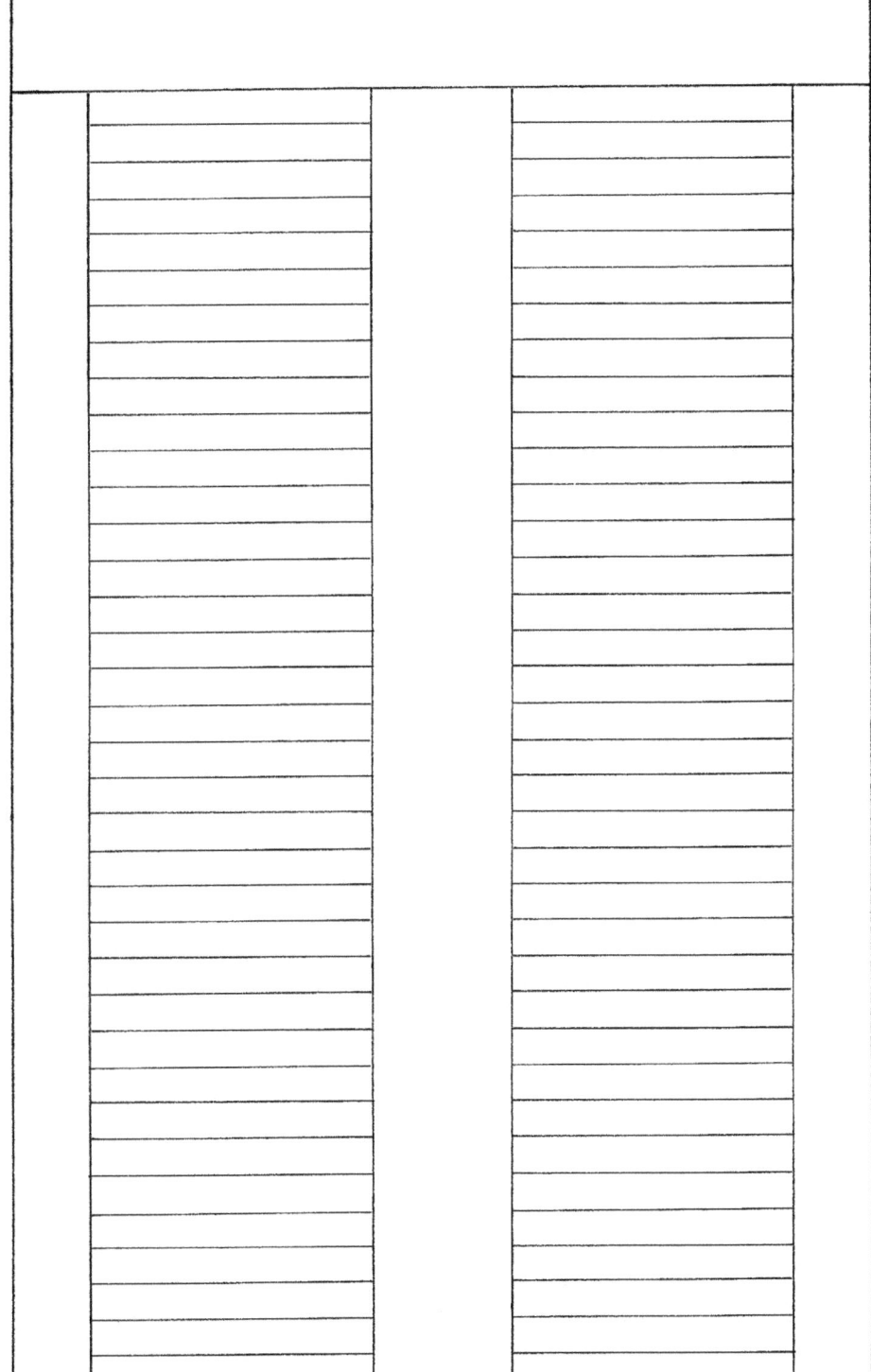

Template 12 24 circles

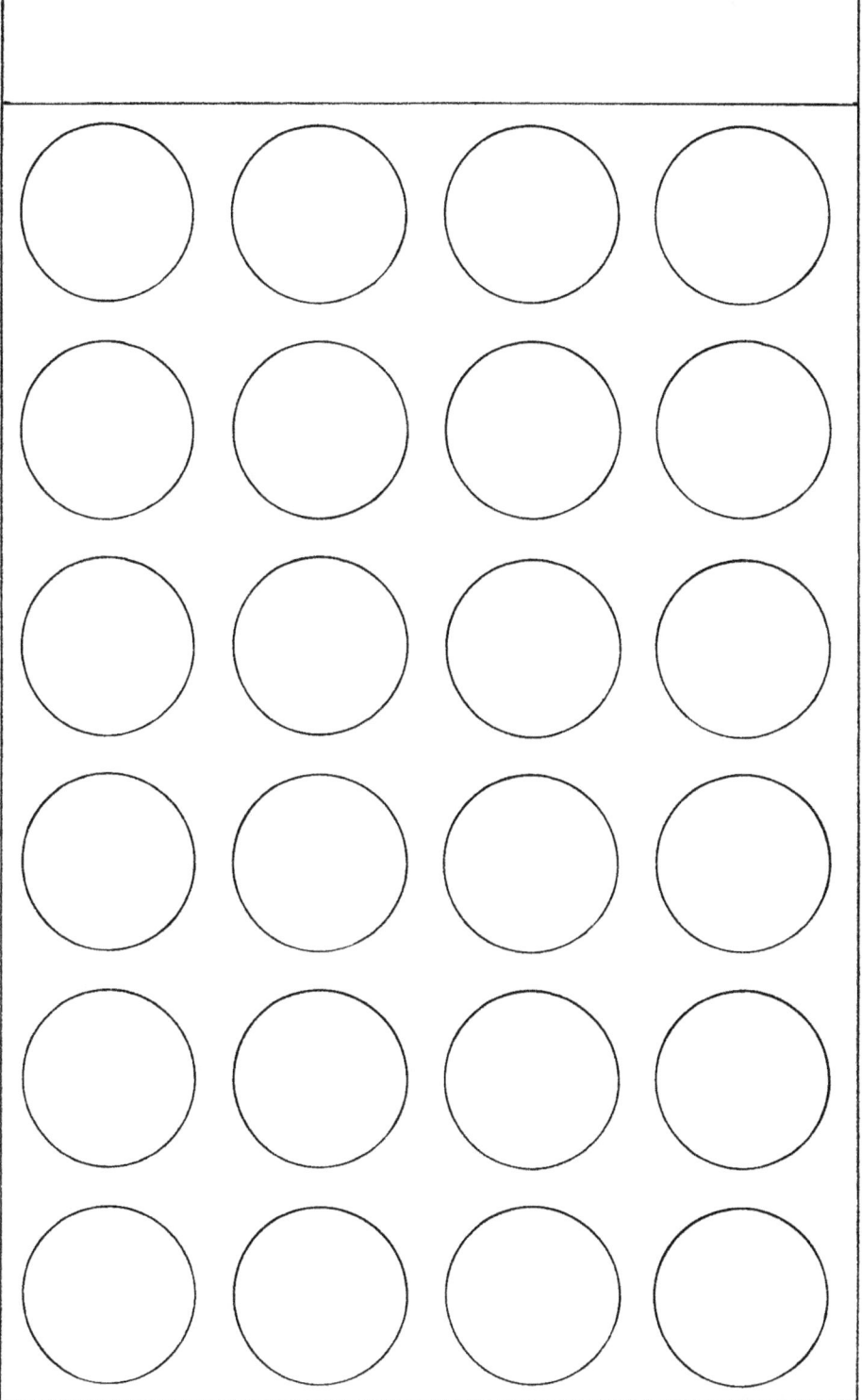

Template 13  9 lines of 12 squares

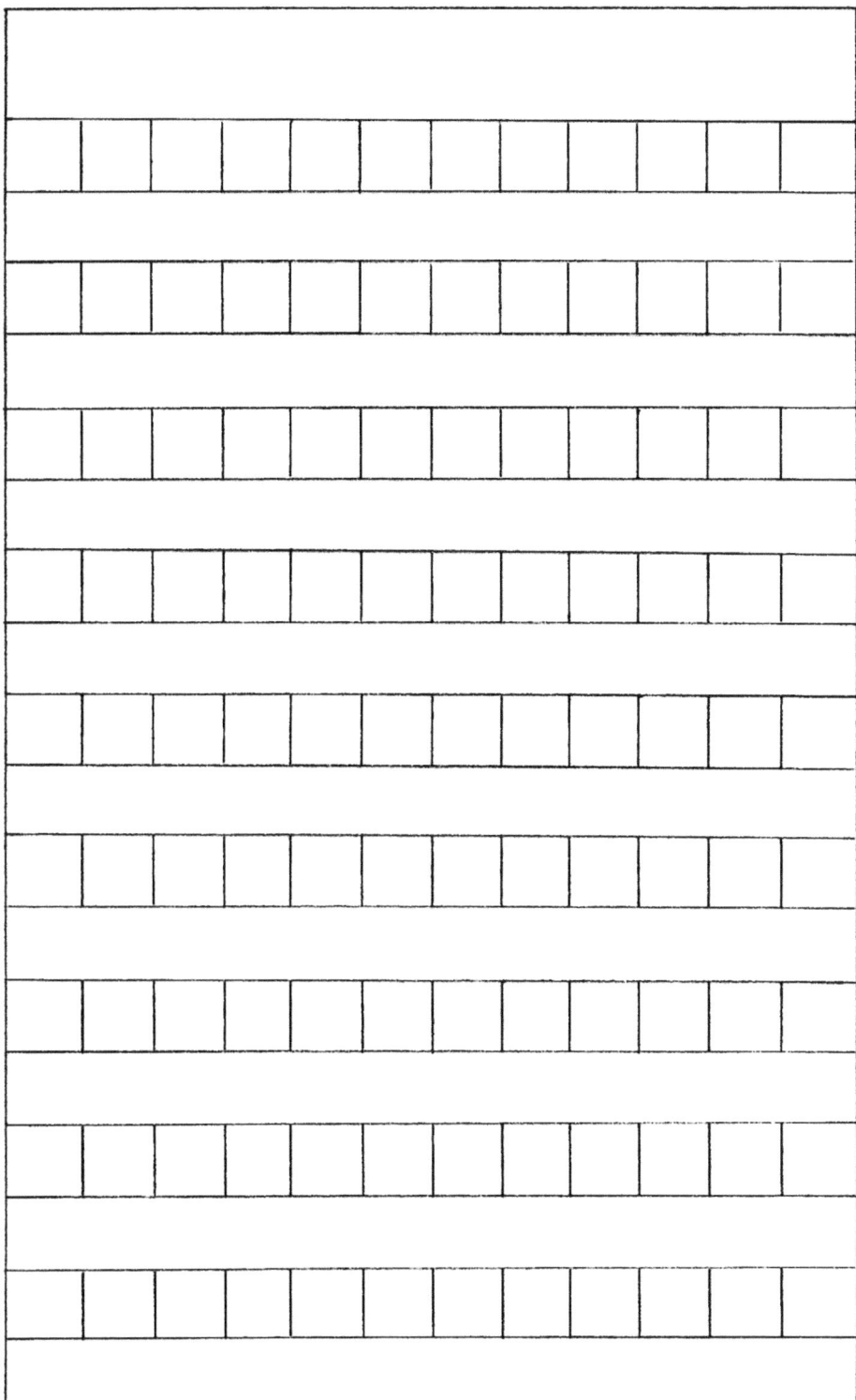

Template 14  36 spaces

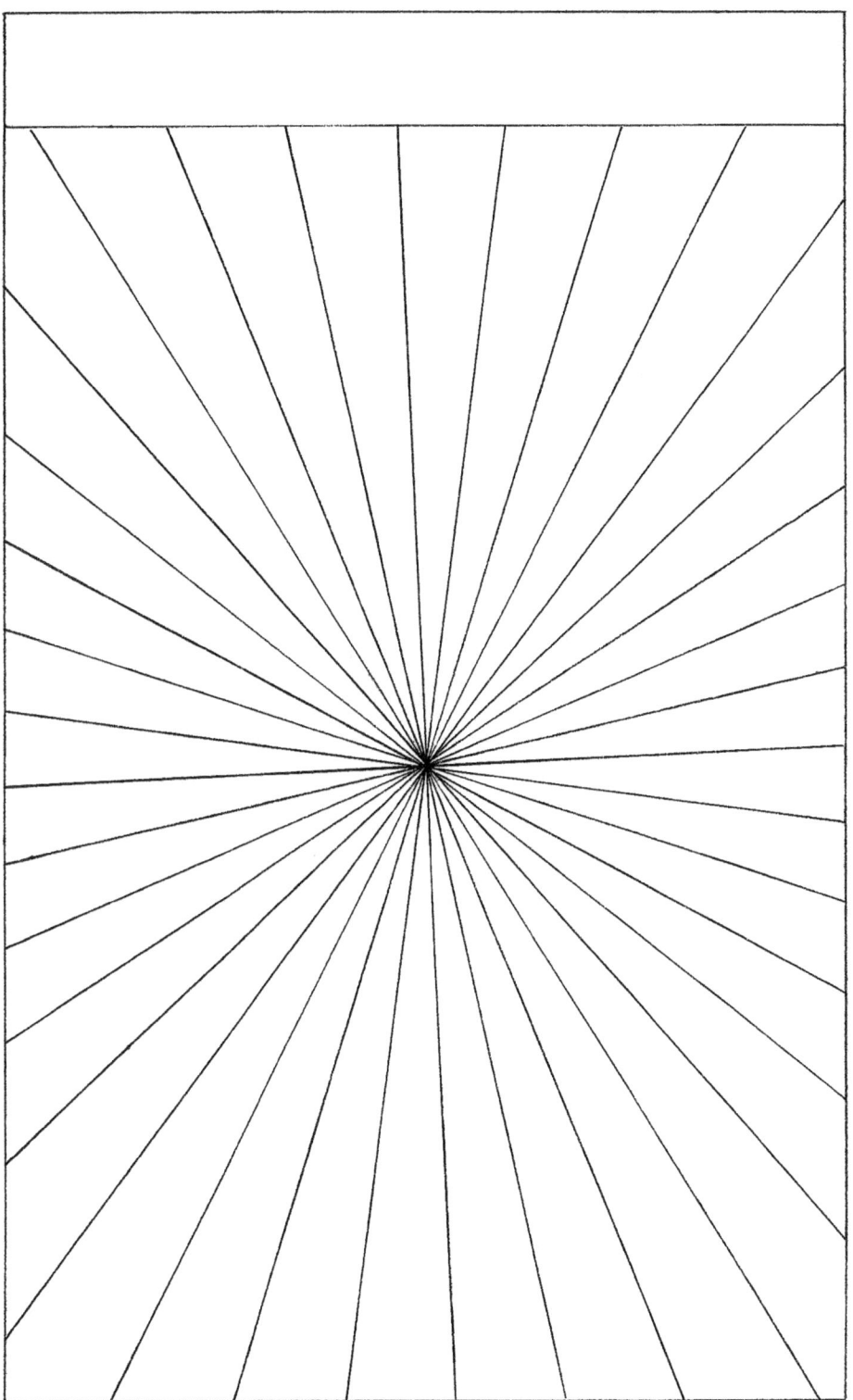

Template 15  1 bcolor Wheel of 36 spaces+ 4 quarters of 9 spaces

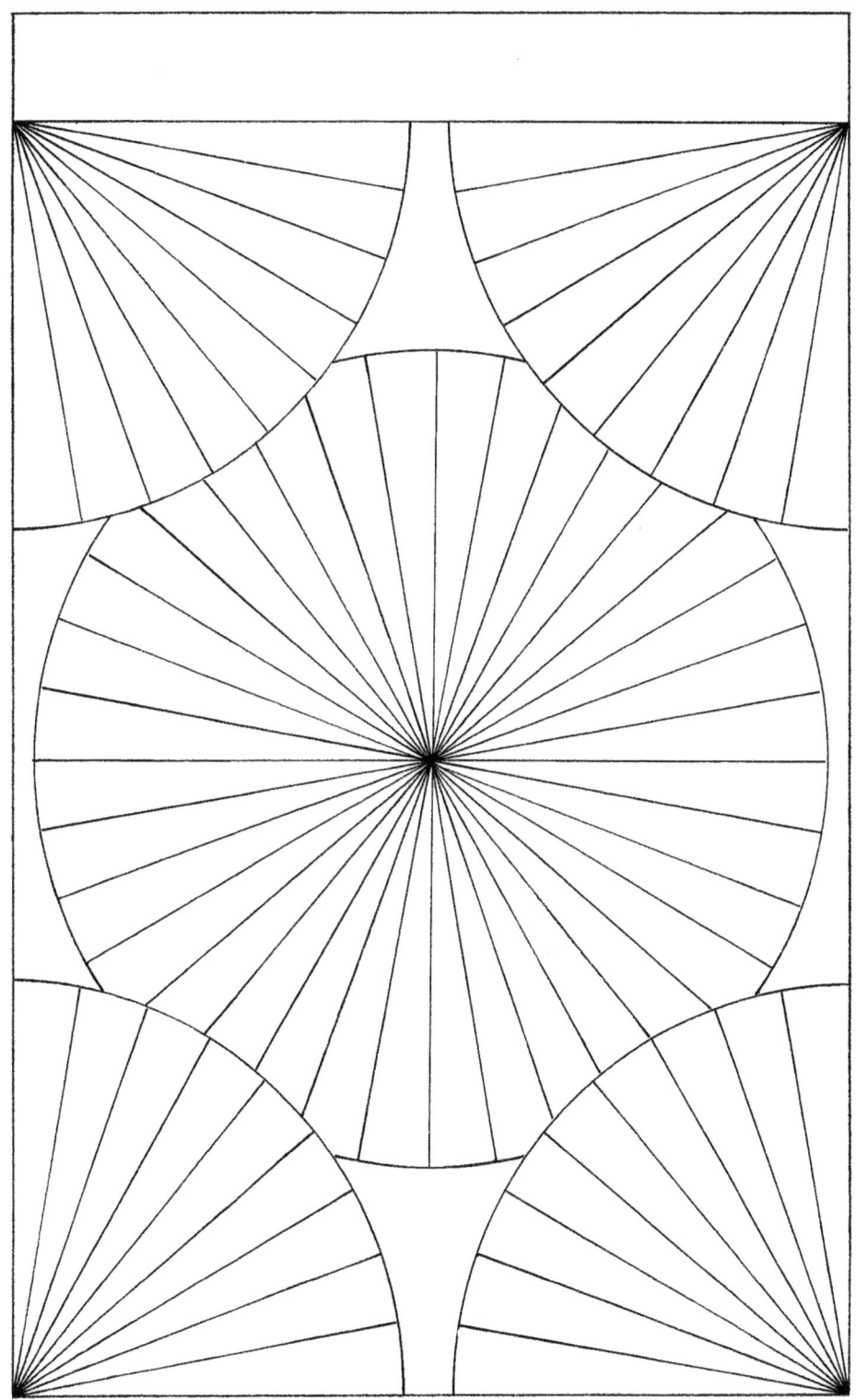

Template 1 Big Color Wheel 2x 72 spaces

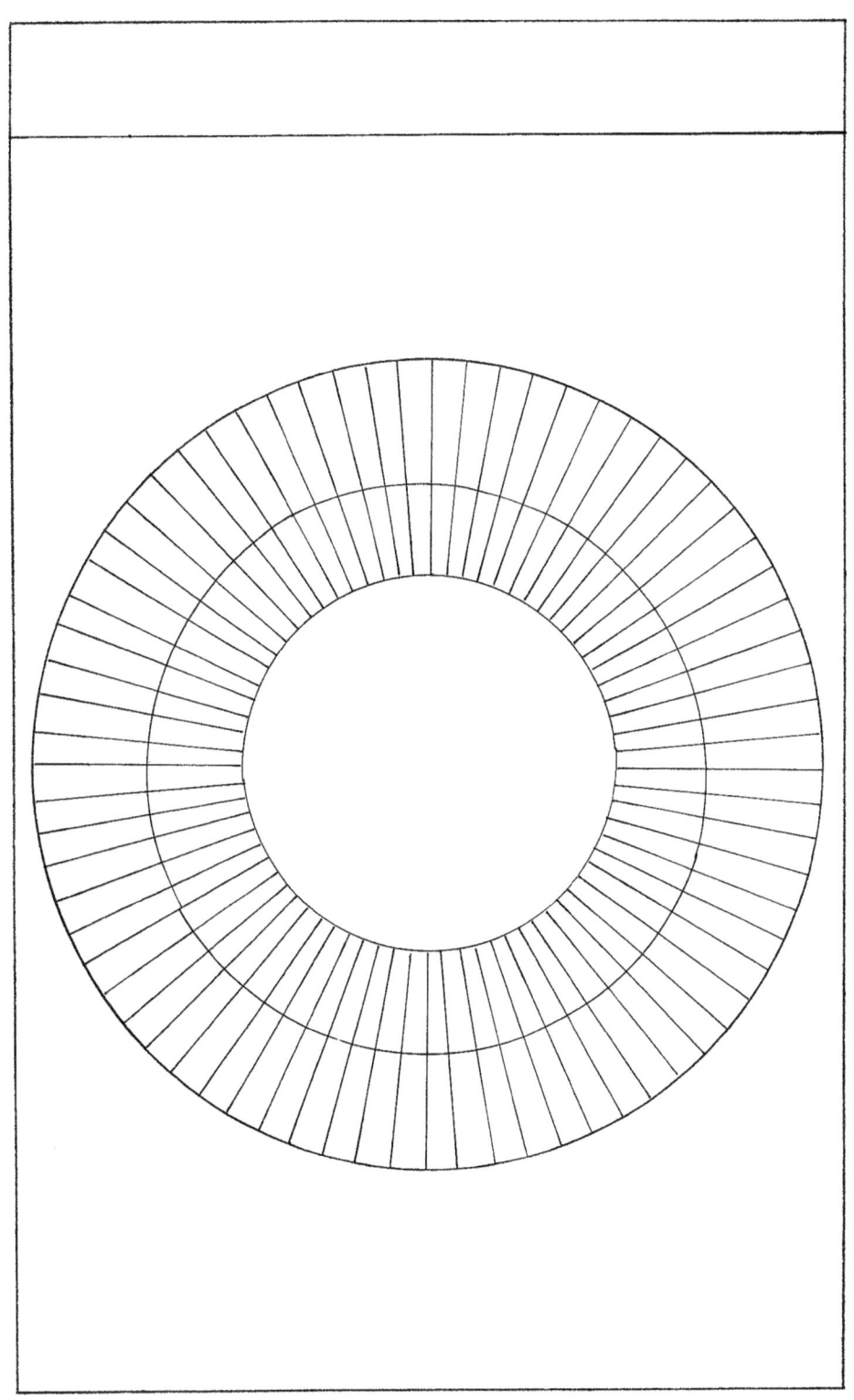

Template 2 Big Color Wheel 36 spaces

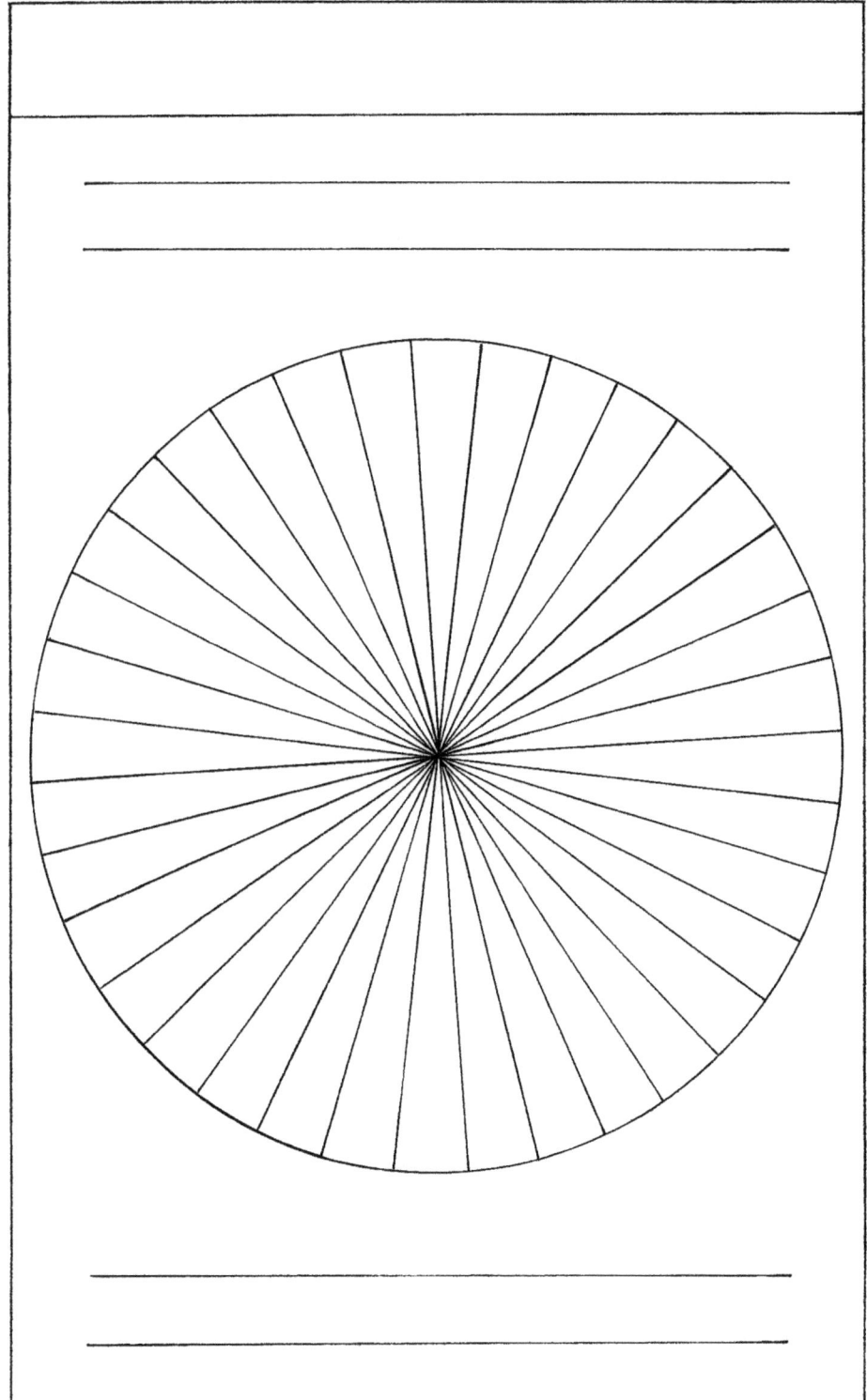

Template 3 Big Color Wheel 2x18 spaces

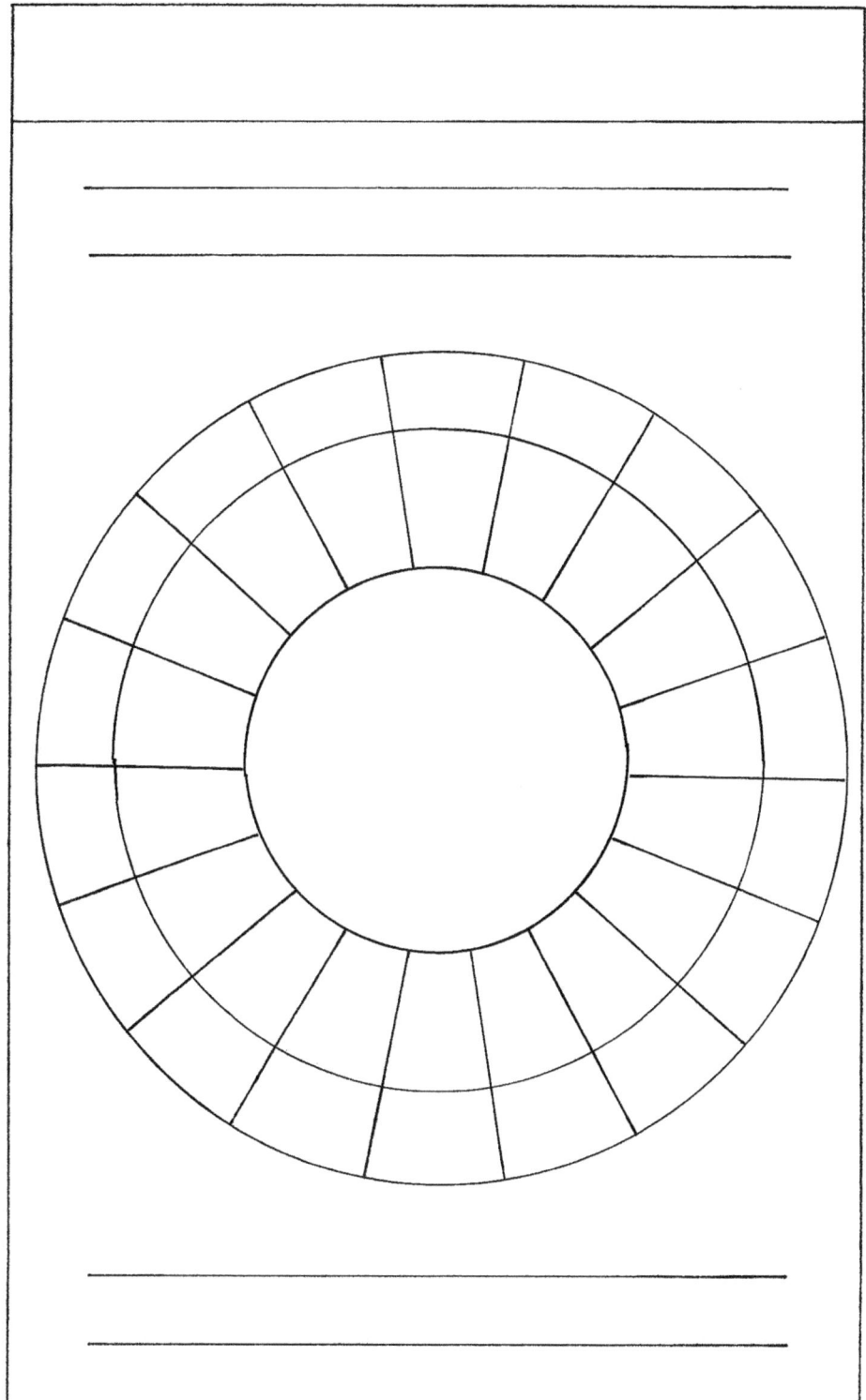

Template 4 Big Color Wheel 36 spaces

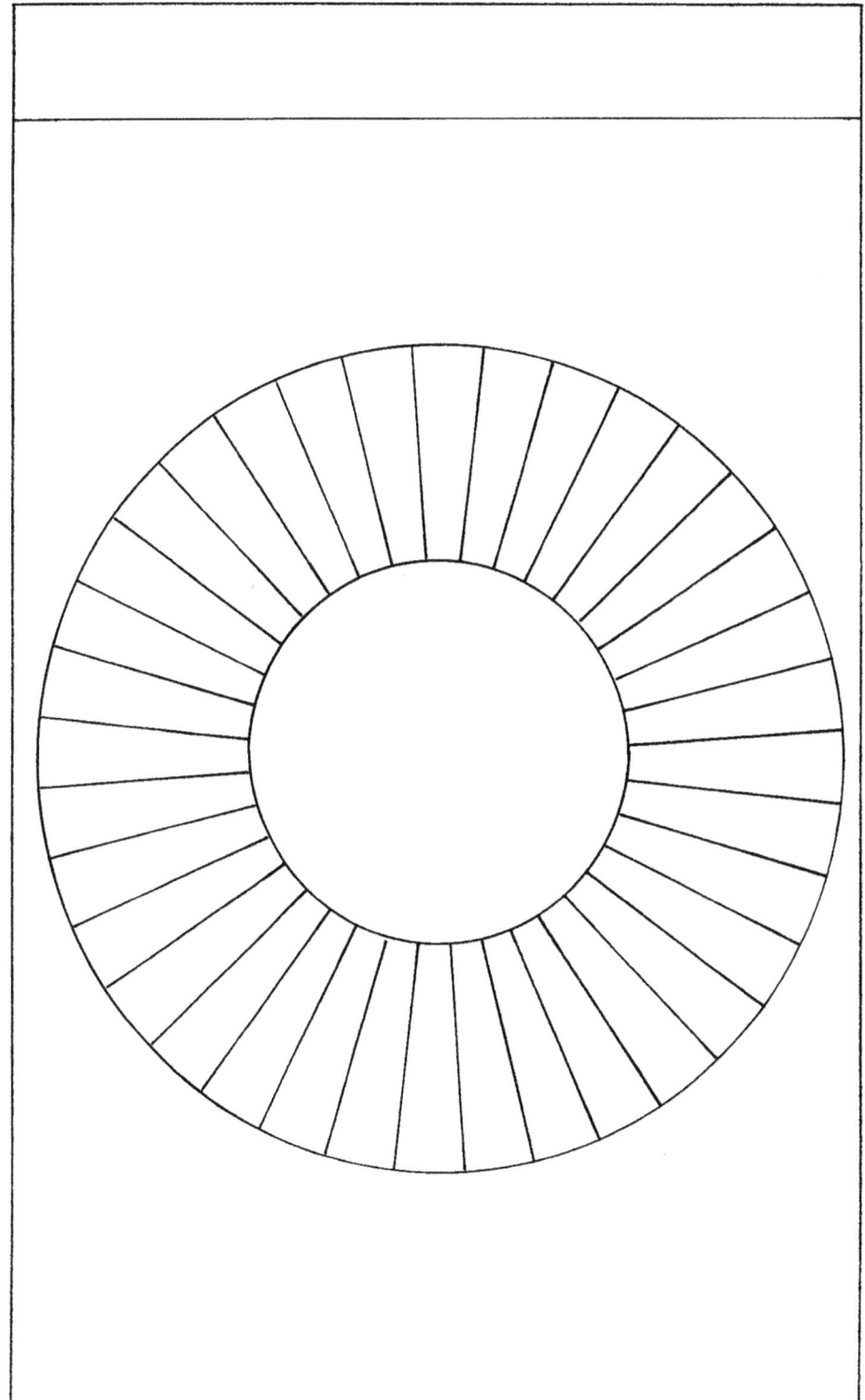

Template 5 15 blogs of 6 spaces

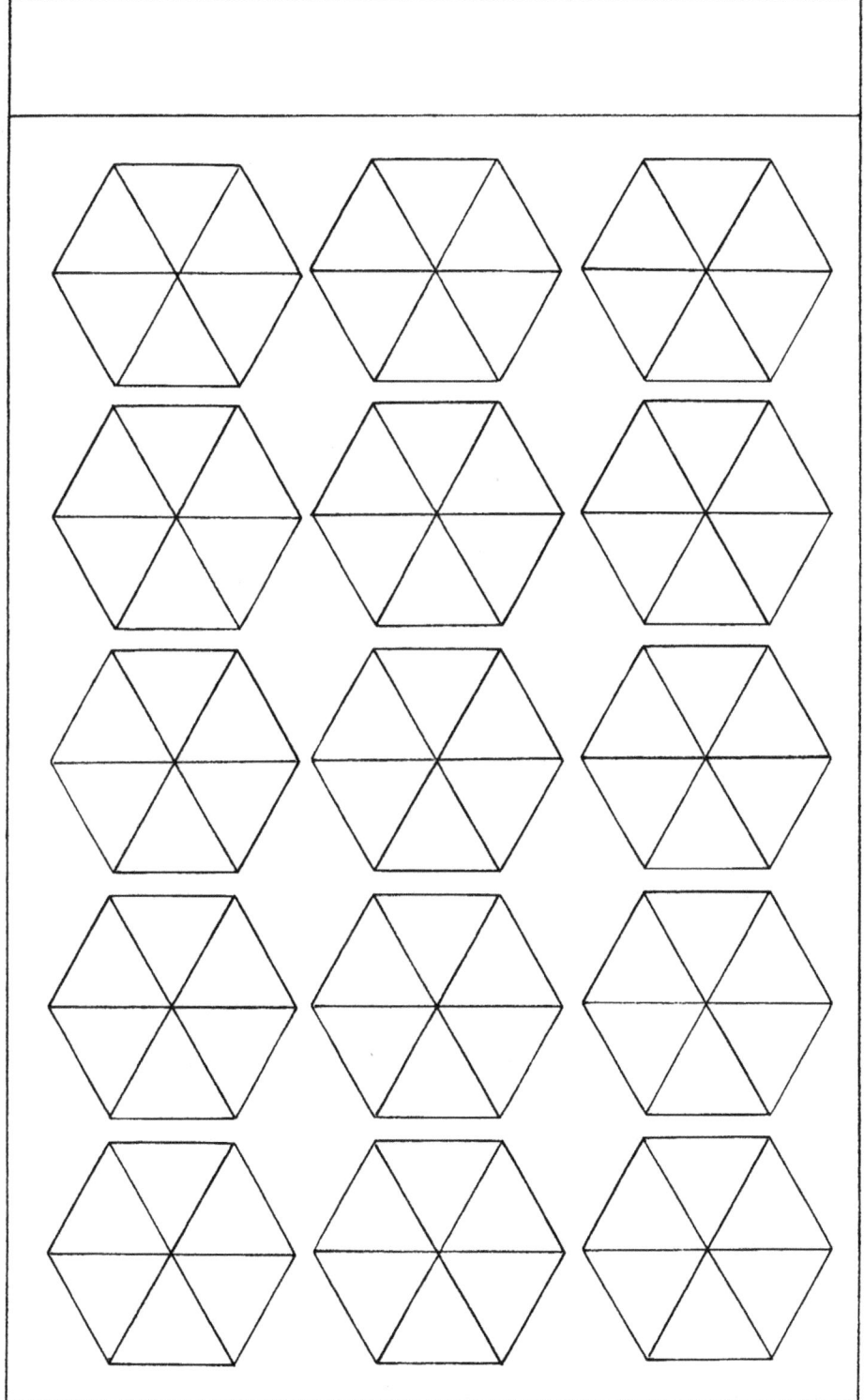

Template 6 6 squares of 4x6 spaces

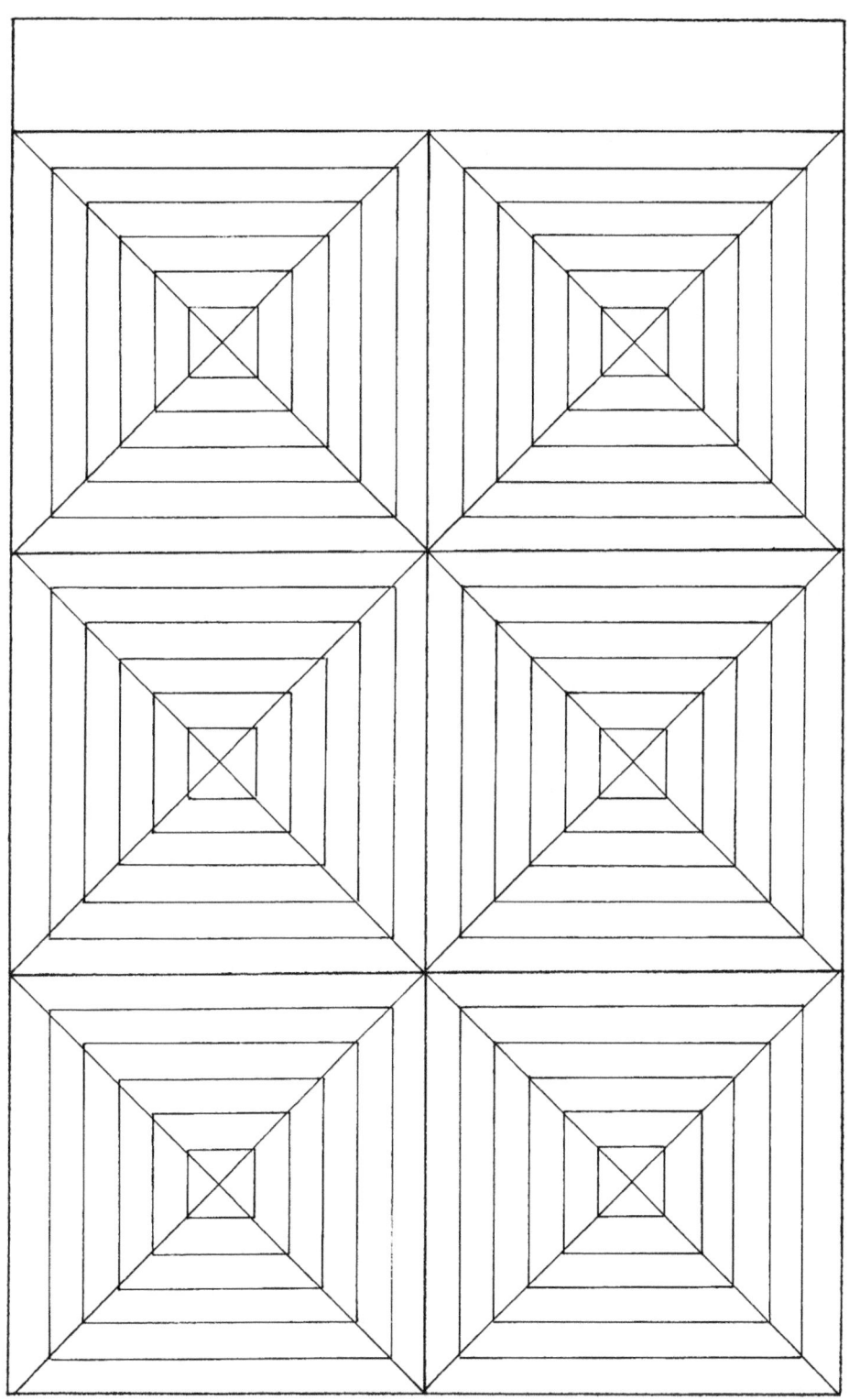

# Template 7 endless possibilities

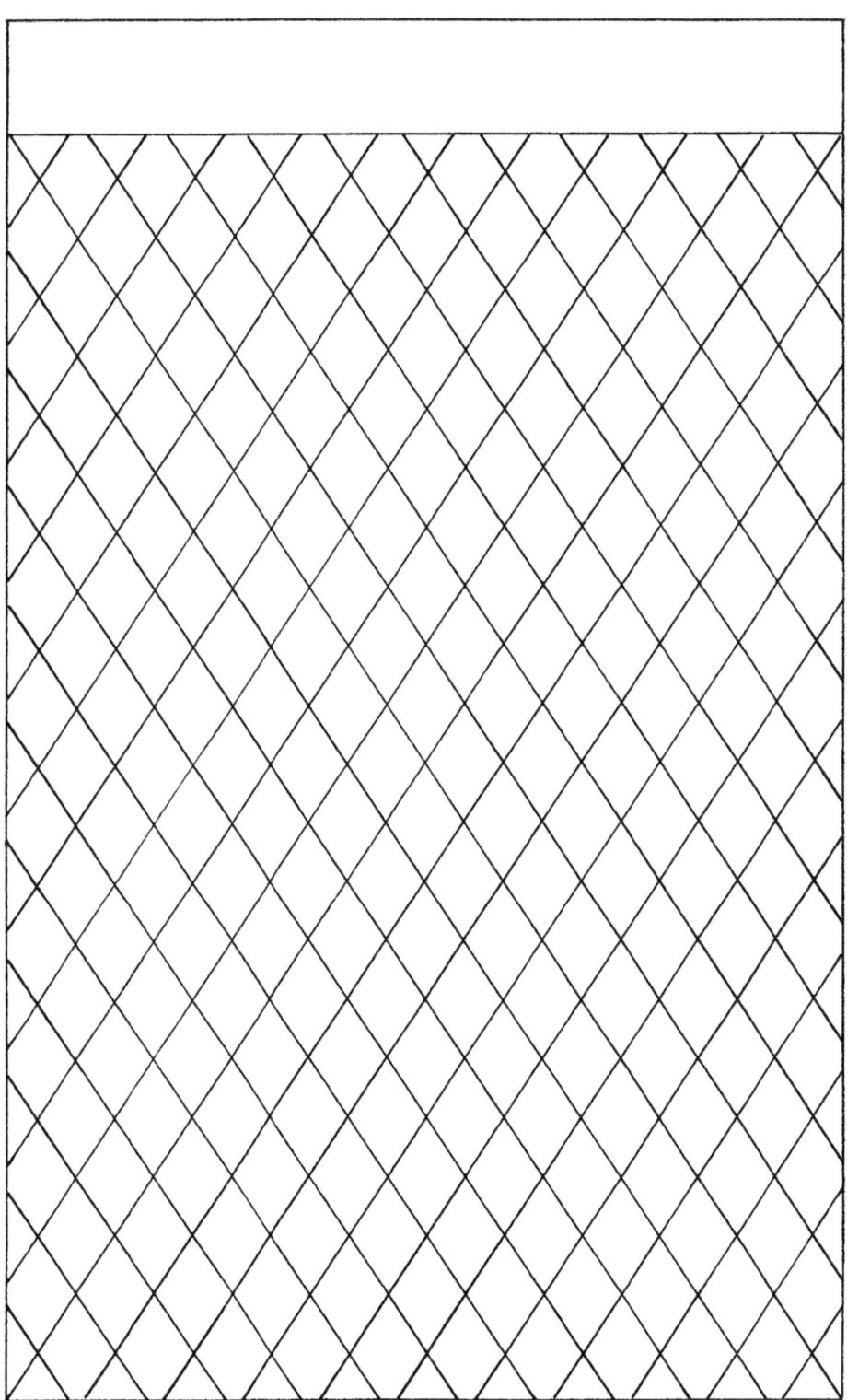

Template 8 6 lines of 32 spaces

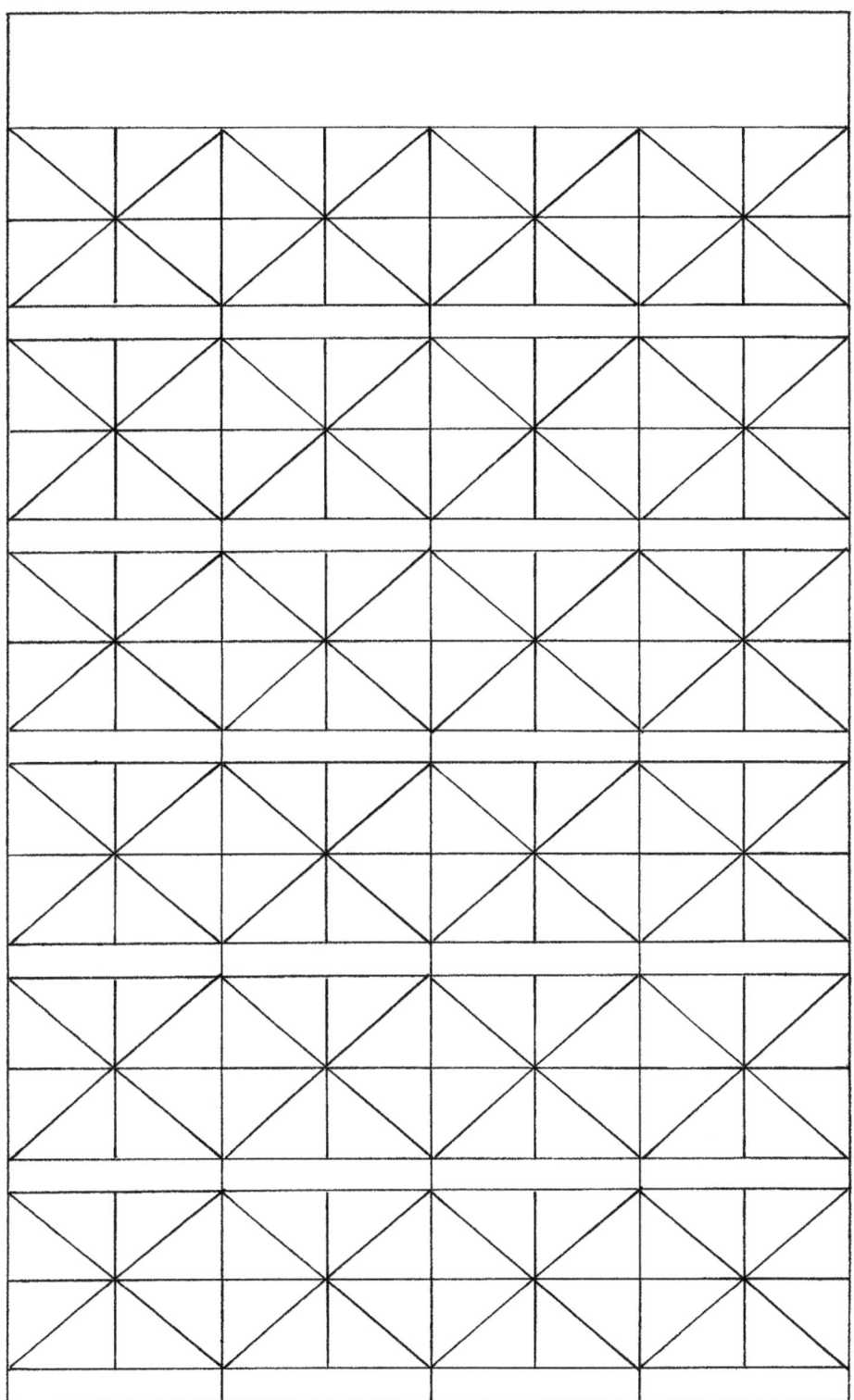

Template 9 6 lines of 24 spaces

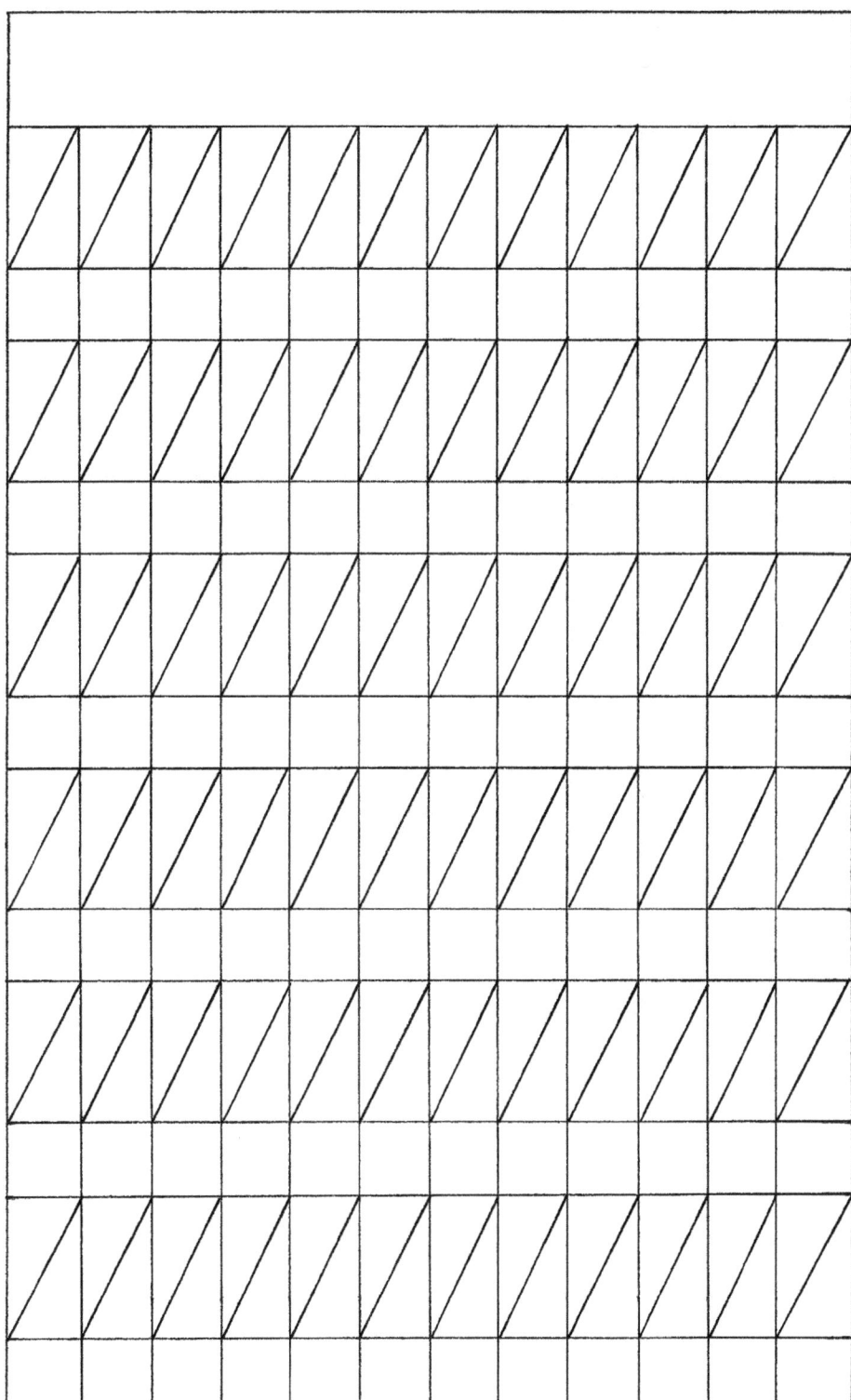

Template 10 Color Wheel 12 spaces

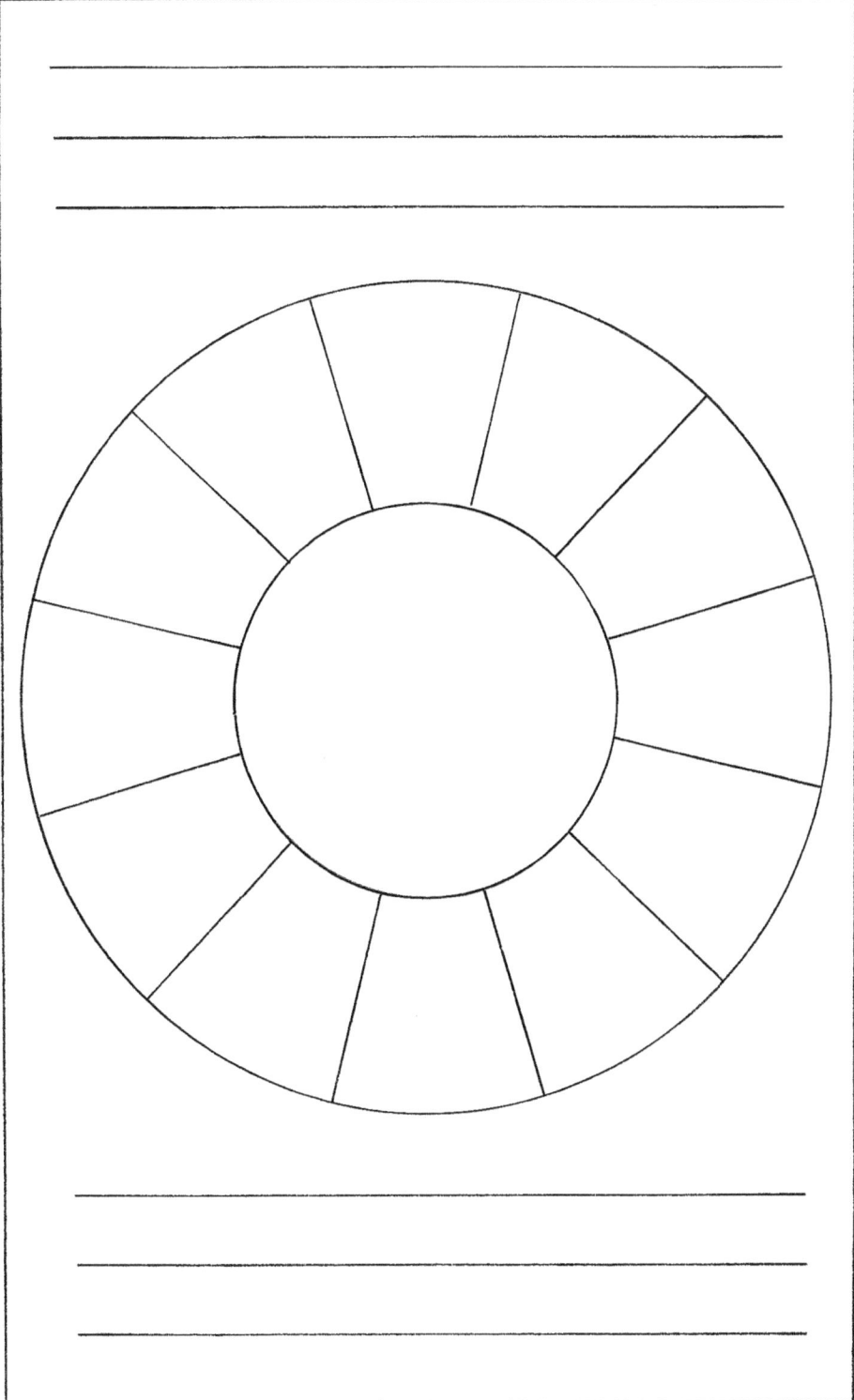

Template 11 2 rows of 36 spaces

# Template 12 24 circles

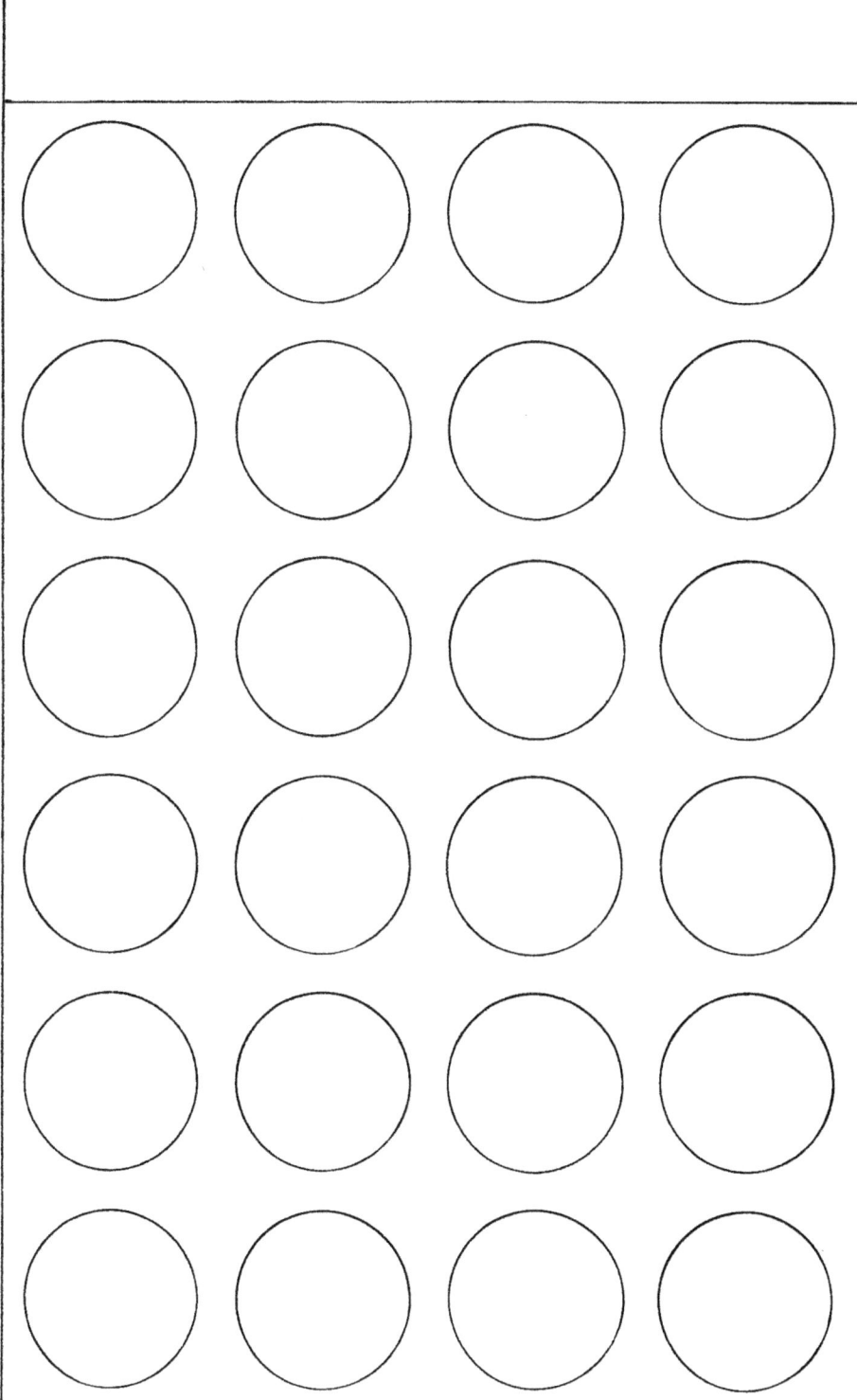

Template 13  9 lines of 12 squares

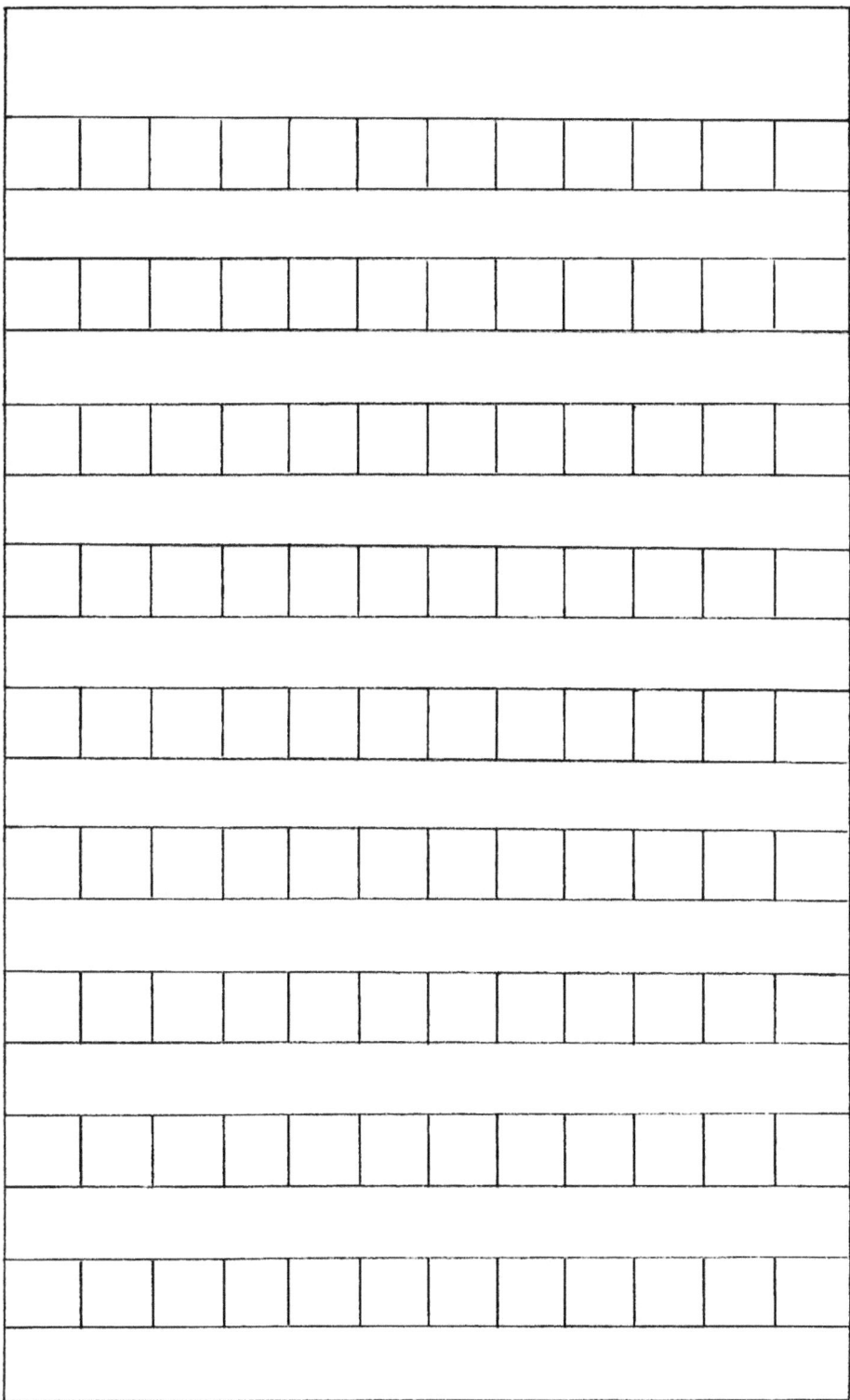

Template 14  36 spaces

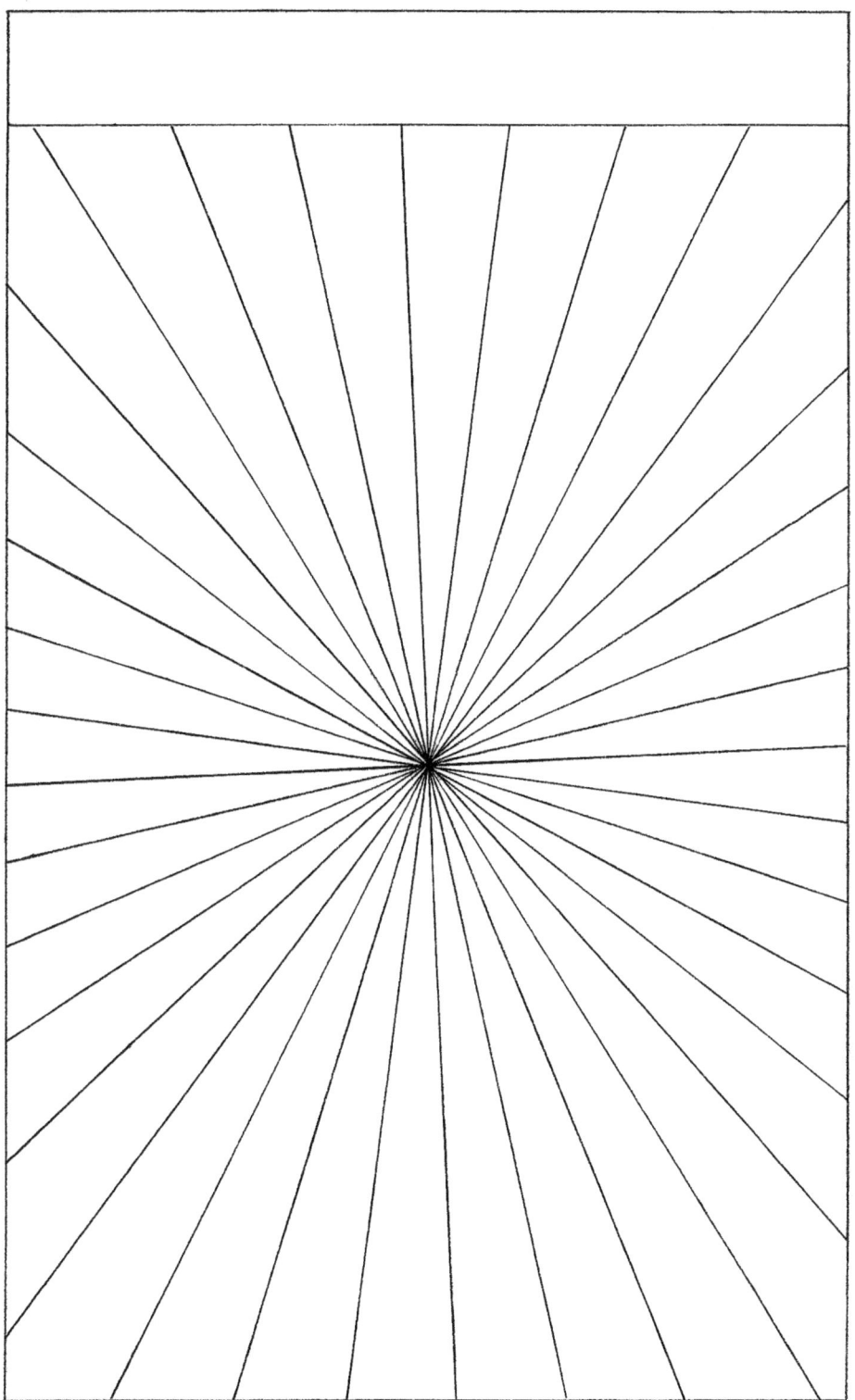

Template 15  1 bcolor Wheel of 36 spaces+ 4 quarters of 9 spaces

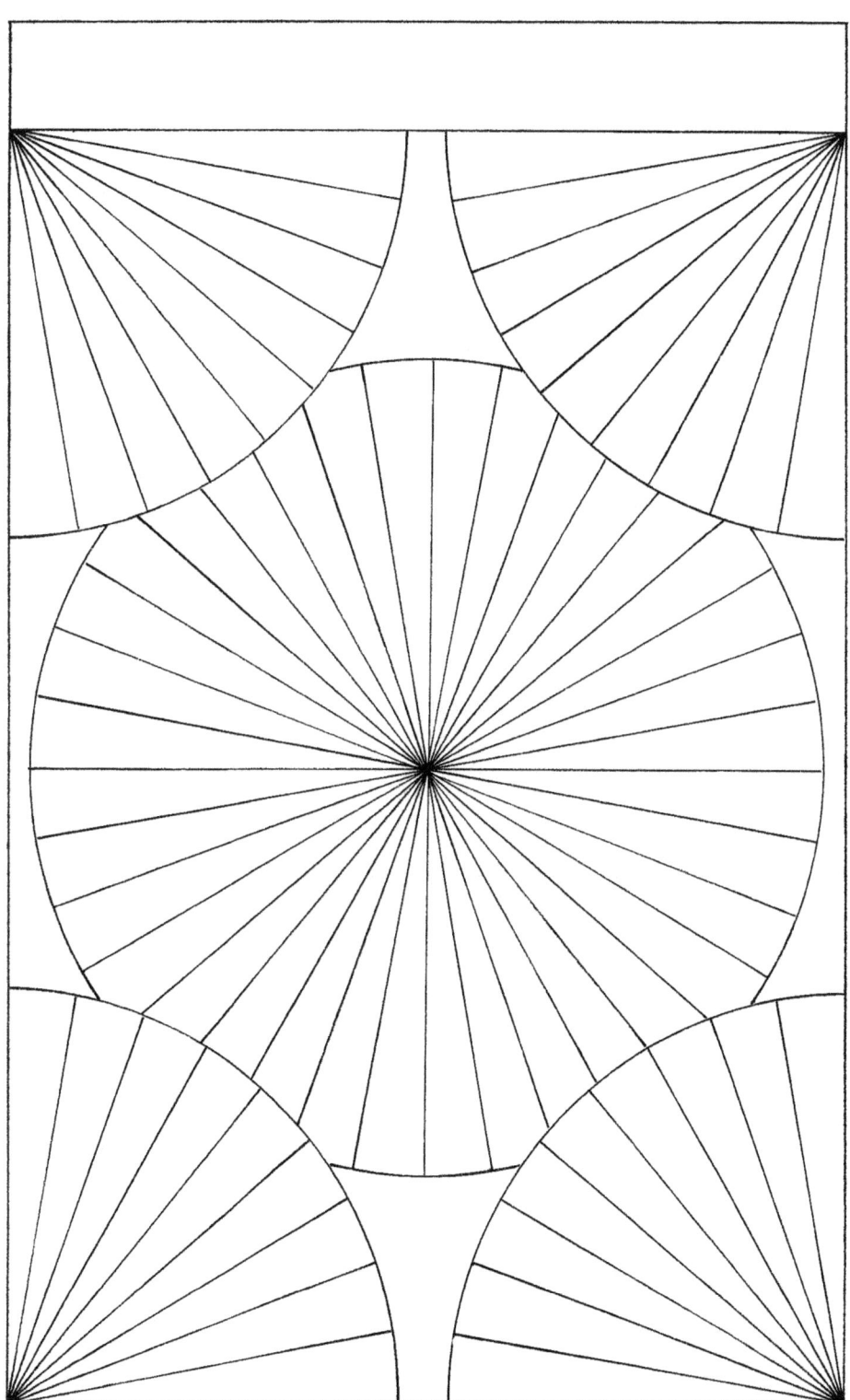

www.ingramcontent.com/pod-product-compliance
Lightning Source LLC
Chambersburg PA
CBHW070254230526
45470CB00002B/597